CLOSE PROTECTION
Luxury & Hostile Environments

Orlando Wilson

Truth Only Has Few Friends
Imam Hussain (as)

Close Protection: Luxury & Hostile Environments Copyright © 2017
by Orlando Wilson. All Rights Reserved.

All rights reserved. No part of this book may be reproduced in any form or by any electronic or mechanical means including information storage and retrieval systems, without permission in writing from the author. The only exception is by a reviewer, who may quote short excerpts in a review.

Cover designed by Orlando Wilson

Orlando Wilson
Visit my website at www.risks-incorporated.com

ISBN-9781980900382

CONTENTS

Introduction 1
The Close Protection & 3
Bodyguard Business 3
Drivers & Bodyguards... Why I don't trust many of them!! 5
Life Skills 7
Escorts & Formations 11
Protective Surveillance 16
Advance Security 19
Staying in a Hotel 21
Attending Events 24
Attending Meetings 28
Close Protection & Personal Security in Hostile Crowds 32
Killing with Kindness 34
The Sex Business 40
Counter-Surveillance Considerations 44
Electronic Surveillance 52
Secrecy 56
Intelligence Gathering 59
Threat Assessments (TA) 63
The Problems of International Training Projects 81
Considerations for Self-Defense 88
First Aid Considerations 100
Traveling with Guns & International Self-Defense 104
Gun Addiction... 108
It could ruin you Masculinity! 108
Tactical Gear List & 111
Considerations for SHTF 111
Countering Snipers 117
Reconnaissance Operations 128
Counter Attack Operations 133
Bombs & Improvised Explosive Device Incidents 139
Orlando Wilson 155

Risks
incorporated

Introduction

The contents of this book are drawn from my experiences in the close protection, security and investigations industry over the last 29 years. What I am providing here is the real-world perspective, not the classroom or perfect world perspective.

I have always questioned what I have been taught, which has got me into plenty of arguments over the years, but without questioning things how they can be improved and refined. I have been very lucky because I have been able to work on many diverse taskings in many diverse palaces and have been able to see what works and what does not. I tell my student's and people to question everything, especially in today's world where fake news and social media outlets are all pushing their agendas and selling products. In the real-world, away from the tacticool entertainment world you need what works and what does not as your life and others can depend on it.

Many people's view of a close protection operative is a big martial arts expert. This stereotype is a widely held misconception. The real professional in the industry is someone who identifies and prevents any situations that could be potentially dangerous to them, their loved ones or clients from happening.

Unarmed combat and shooting skills are only part of what you may need to know, but these skills people over emphasis as they are a lot more interesting and exciting the essentials like planning or threat assessments. If you plan your personal security properly and take the necessary precautions, you will, hopefully, never have to apply your shooting or unarmed combat skills. When you consider all the things that can harm you, the threat from shooting is not at the top of the list, you are more likely to be involved in a car accident or suffer from some form of food poisoning.

You must learn to identify all threats in your everyday life, the protection business in 24/7 and if you can't look after yourself, how can you look after others? When you learn the skills taught in this manual, apply them in your everyday life. Do a threat assessment on yourself and work out what threats you are under and make the necessary plans to minimize them. Not all the subjects in this manual will apply to everyone, so when you read through the manual take the information which is relevant to you and adapt it to your personal requirements. Just as everyone is different, so are their security requirements- use this manual as a guide to plan your own procedures. Once you have compiled your procedures you should then keep them as confidential as possible, this is a way of life, not a job.

I put an emphasis on planning to avoid potential problems. Over the years I have had people attend my courses who wanted close quarter combat training as they work or are traveling to a potentially hostile location. When I ask them how they will be getting from the airport to their hotel 95% haven't even thought about it. Airports are a choice location for organized or express kidnappings. How will you know if your licensed taxi driver is taking you to your hotel or to another location, did you research the routes before you travel? Do know if his license is legitimate or someone else's with his picture on it; have your seen examples of legitimate licenses? What will you do when the taxi stops, and two kidnappers get in with 9mm pistols; shoot you way out of it? Most people forget that in a lot of countries firearms are strictly regulated and the chances a tourist or business visitor can take or carry a firearm are extremely slim. It makes more sense to do your research and avoid easily avoidable problems rather than ending dead in a ghetto back alley somewhere or in a 3rd world prison because you took a gun off and shot a kidnapper who turned out to be a police officer!

The information in this manual has been compiled from my twenty-nine plus years of operational experience and also from that of my close associates. Our experience has been gained while working within military, intelligence, police units and in the international commercial security sector. Our major asset is our diverse and constant operational experience that helps us understand firsthand the problems that can be encountered and how to deal with them with sensible solutions. We live and work in the real world!

This book would be too large if I included all the information required. So, for further reading on related topics check my other books on travel security, home and office security, kidnap and ransom and tactical pistol training on Amazon @ www.amazon.com/author/orlandowilson

Orlando Wilson
4/25/18

The Close Protection & Bodyguard Business

I tell people I would never recommend the close protection/bodyguard business to anyone as a career, but personally I would do nothing else. I have been working in the commercial security industry internationally since 1993 after I left the British Army. In this chapter I will talk about the close protection industry but over the years a lot of my business has also come from security and tactical training as well as corporate investigations. If close protection services are provided properly they combine a lot of different skill sets, sadly most of the supposed professionals in the industry don't seem to understand this....

I've provided services to a wide variety of clientele most of whom have been excellent to work with mainly because I don't just take any clients. Providing close protection/bodyguard services to a client is a lot different that providing regular security services, it's a lot more of a personal service. I have seen companies in London piss off clients because they treated them, their families and homes the same as if they were providing security for an office block. This was down to bad management personnel with no commercial close protection experience.

Because close protection is a personal business in which you can end up spending a lot of time in close proximity with your clients, there has to be a rapport. If the bodyguard and the client do not get along then you're going to have problems. The client's lifestyle needs to be taken into consideration when deciding if you or one of your people can work with them. Problems can come from let's say clients that like the night club scene and can range from alcohol abuse, recreation drugs or sexual partners they decide to pick up. These things are part of life and you need to take them into consideration with your assessments and plans. Don't be prude! I personally tend to stick with the clients with issues in the more edgy locations but know plenty of personnel who are at home in the nightclubs of London and Paris.

As for those providing close protection and bodyguard services the quality ranges from excellent to liabilities on legs. Sadly, most fall into the latter category. The main qualities a good close protection operative/bodyguard need are intelligence and to be able to communicate with people from all backgrounds. People put an emphasis on guns and martial arts because they want to be Hollywood tough guys, right? But they forget the emphasis needs to be on avoiding the problem, violent situations mean people get hurt, killed, go to jail and in the U.S. most likely sued! Saying that you need to be street wise and be able to protect yourself and clients, if you worried about such things as a broken nose or scuffed knuckles you're defiantly in the wrong business.

I have had students attend my course who have been through other supposed close protection schools and were far less capable than many novices because they had been miss-trained for commercial close protection. U.S./Israeli government agency style techniques don't work when the client is traveling with 1 bodyguard... Try walking around a busy shopping mall in Dubai or anywhere for that matter in a fixed 4-man formation... PSD techniques work in Iraq and Afghanistan but you're not going to be walking around Ibiza with an AK or M-4... Understanding budgets and international laws is also part of your planning and preparation but many in the industry are oblivious to such things.

One of the biggest problems with the close protection industry is bad management, many of those running security companies have no experience of performing close protection or security duties themselves. They bullshit their way into contracts and their only concern is billing the clients for the maximum they can get out of them, but this is what business is about right? It's all good until things go wrong and in the serious world of close protection that means people get hurt or go to jail. I pity the clients that hire what they believe is a highly experience company when in fact they've been sold a lie. This happens a lot, so to all potential clients make sure you do your due diligence and don't believe the sales pitches and glossy brochures!

Drivers & Bodyguards... Why I don't trust many of them!!

The quality of bodyguards and trained security drivers can vary greatly and in most places the standards are low. I have seen many clients over the years being driven around protected by guys who just happen to have firearms permits or were moonlighting local police, who for all these clients knew were working for the criminals also. Several years ago, I went with two American clients to an island in the Caribbean where at the time the crime and kidnapping rates were high. My clients were dealing with a European company on the island that were to provide them with security, but they want me to go along as they were not getting a positive feeling from the trip and arrangements. So, I arrange extra trusted local armed security personnel and an armored vehicle to accompany us.

The population of the island is predominantly of African descent, so my clients and I had no real chance of blending in. My business partner met us with our local security guys inside of the airport, as there is always a high risk when leaving airports because you are being channeled. We then went to look for the security personnel who had come to pick up my clients from the European company they were dealing with. This company's bodyguard was easy to spot as he was the only white guy outside of the airport holding a sign with mine and my client's names on. At this stage the bodyguard did not know I was providing security for my clients. As we were going to his vehicle I informed him that I had my own local security personnel who would be following us back to our hotel. As we drove through the city my guys in a black SUV drove very aggressively and stayed close to our vehicle. When we got to our hotel the bodyguard told us to stay in the car as he thought we were being followed and was going to check the car out behind us; we were being followed, by my security people, he had not been listening when I informed him of this.

This bodyguard who I know must have done at least five years' European military service and I expect at least one specialist training course made two very big mistakes that could have led to serious problems. One, he stood out at the airport and by having mine and my client's full names on a piece of paper was letting everyone know who we were. If a criminal with an internet capable cell phone had Googled my client's names they would have seen, they were worth kidnapping. Two, why did he wait until we got back to our hotel to check out my security guy's car that was following us. If he thought they were a threat he should have asked us if we knew them, taken evasive action or stayed mobile and called for support; which this company claimed to have on standby. If my guys had been criminals, this bodyguard had just taken them to our place of residence. I still don't know what he was going to achieve by going and checking my guys out at the hotel as he had no authority to stop and question anyone, he was also carrying a firearm which he could not really legally have a permit to carry.

This is a good example of supposedly trained security personnel not knowing or caring about what they are doing. I expect they had not had any problems or though no one would target them and had relaxed to a point of being ineffective, this happens if security teams are not well managed. The other funny thing was as we were leaving our hotel to go to my client's first meeting with this company the car they supplied got a flat tire and it had no break down kit. So, we transferred everyone to my local guy's vehicle and left the driver to deal with the flat. We let the bodyguard sit in the front as we felt sorry for him; he was not having a good day!

If you are going to use local drivers and security personnel try to get them some training or at least go through your basic emergency plans with them. If you are under a threat, let them know that the threat also applies to them and their families. Make sure they take the relevant security measures and are always vigilant for the threat of criminal surveillance. Your driver should never stand outside the vehicle when you approach it, have a safety signal with them and do not approach the vehicle until they give the signal. The driver should always be behind the wheel with the engine running and ready to make a quick escape in the case of an emergency. On arrival at your destination the driver should remain behind the wheel of the vehicle; it would be the job of the bodyguard to open your door, if required. You should always know where the driver is and how to contact them. If the driver is not 100% trusted only inform them of routes or destinations just before or after the journey has started and do not give them any long-term schedules.

Life Skills...

As I have said, I have been involved in the security industry internationally since leaving the British Army in 1993 and things have changed dramatically since then... Sure, the basic physical tactics, techniques and procedures have remained more or less the same but, with the development of the internet communications, logistics and networking is in a completely different world. Sadly, though there are still many still stuck in the 1990's.

One of the first large investigations I completed when I started working for myself in the mid 90's was to locate a fishing trawler in the far East of Russia... This entailed getting contacts to 1. Locate the vessel 2. Take and develop photos 3. Send to Moscow 4. Fax me the photos and report from Moscow 5. Originals were sent to me via FedEx 6. I forwarded to the client... This job took about 3 weeks if I remember right... These days as soon as the vessel was located we could stream real-time video to the client via a smart phone...

I find it funny how many people seeking work and quite a few working in the close protection, investigations industry have completed many tacticool courses and maybe licensed in numerous locations but are still lacking the basic soft skills required to be able to complete the basic of tasks... I class these basic skills as life skills that apply to virtually everyone, especially those who work for themselves.

These skills include:
- Must be able to use a computer or smartphone
- Must be able to use various messengers
- Must be able to write a report
- Must be able to take viewable photos and video
- Must be able to plan a route and use maps – physical & digital
- Must be able to get from one location to another on time, internationally
- Must be able to book flights, hotels and cars internationally
- Must be able to send and receive money internationally

You might the best shot or hardest puncher in the world but if you can't communicate or get from point A to B without drama you're a waste of space. Many of the supposed training experts are more focused on being tacticool instead of teaching real-world skills, this sadly means many trying to join the industry are miss-trained, which can be worse than being untrained. A simple thing like not knowing North from South can lead to issues when looking for locations. Not being able to send funds international can lead to delays in tasks be completed or cancelled...

These are just some thoughts on issues I come across regularly, we should never be dependent on technology, but we need to know how to use it...

Behavior

Your personal behavior and reputation is the most important factor in you gaining regular contracts. There are many people who have attended lots of close protection, firearms and driving courses, etc. but still do not know how to act when working with a client or a professional team. The common downfall of a lot people is their egos; they think because they have done some courses or have some experience that they are better than everyone else. One person once said to me, after they completed a CP course in 1995, that he was trained as a team leader not just a team member! To my knowledge this person to date has only ever been a regular security guard.

These people see themselves as professional bodyguards and have hit the big time because if they are lucky they are looking after a client and get to hang around five-star hotels. I have seen this type of bodyguard walking around the lobby of five-star hotels in London with their radios in shoulder holsters and no jackets on, just to make sure everyone knows they are a bodyguard.

Another downfall and a sign of inexperience is people who overreact to the slightest thing and see threats where there are none. You can't push people out of the way of your client or stand in the road and stop traffic for their vehicle to pull out, and you most definitely can't manhandle your client just because some walks near them. Work to the threat level of the job and blend in with your client and the environment you are working in. Forget the Hollywood black suit, black tie, white shirt and shades bullshit.

If the threat level is high enough and the laws of the country you are in allow it, then you will most probably carry weapons: spray, batons, firearms etc. In UK for example you cannot carry any weapons, but some people do so. I have come across people in UK carrying ASP's, coshes and stun guns, all weapons are banned in UK! If these people are caught carrying illegal weapons by the police, they will be arrested even though some people believe in their small minds that the police will turn a blind eye to them because they are bodyguards. If you are working on a job where there is a threat and can't carry weapons, then you must learn to adapt everyday items. Some people carry large mag-light torches, these are legal but look stupid sticking out from under a suit or dinner jacket in an up-market restaurant or hotel.

It is easy for people to be keen on a job for a few active days, but it takes a different type of person to remain alert and professional over a long period of time. Self-discipline is very important as well as the ability to get on and communicate with others. The last thing you need on a job are people who are always arguing, complaining, back stabbing etc. All this does is bring down the overall morale of the job and in the end the friction in the team will affect the service being supplied to the client. You will find people all the time that will creep up to the client and their close staff and trying to win brownie points. There is a big difference between doing your job and creeping up to the client. Influential and rich people are used to people coming to them for favors or money and usually have little respect for them and will lose respect for you if you do so. The main thing that people forget is that they are just another member of staff to the client. The client can sack their whole security team if they feel like it for one person's mistake, it happens. Your attitude should be to go to work do your job and go home again, stay out of the politics and petty arguments.

Punctuality is another subject not covered on a lot of CP courses but is very important. You should always be 15 minutes early whether it is to relieve another team member or to go out with your client. If you are working a static job it is very annoying to be relieved late, especially if your relief does not have a good reason for doing so. This can cause friction within a team and lead to dismissals. If you are going to be late, for whatever reason, inform the person you are relieving or your client ASAP.

Appearance is an extremely important and your clothes should always be clean and neat. If you are dressed immaculately you will appear to exude confidence and strength and people will assume that you have the knowledge and the ability to take care of yourself. You should always dress to the client's requirements; this usually means in a suit, but some clients prefer their security to wear casual clothes. Suits should be of a dark color; a conservative fine pin stripe is preferable to a fashion suit.

You should always get a big double-breasted jacket that can be done up and conceal what equipment you are carrying on your person, i.e. radios, phones, note books/diaries, first aid kit, weapons, extra ammo, etc. If you are carrying weapons, you will usually keep your jacket undone. A double-breasted jacket will conceal what is under you jacket better than a single breasted one. An oversized unbuttoned jacket is a good indication that someone is armed.

Your shirts should always be clean. Try not to always wear white shirts- most people who wear suits all the time wear colored shirts, dress to blend in with your environment. In hot weather, colored shirts have the advantage of not showing sweat or dirt so much as white shirts. Where possible, always keep a spare clean shirt to hand and change when possible. Your tie should be silk, it should be a darker color than your shirt, and the knot should be of medium size, but this size should match the collar.

You need to wear belt and braces; belts are a necessity for carrying radios or weapons. Braces will keep your trousers up with all the equipment you've got on your belt. Black shoes will go with any color suit except brown, tie shoes are preferable, no buckles and no combat boots. Socks should be dark in color and should match the suit. The only expectable jewelry are wedding bands. If you have tattoos they should be covered.

If you smoke, never smoke when you are on duty or around your client, even if the client smokes. Don't scratch, pick your nose, chew gum, etc. when with your client. Hygiene is very important when you are working with other people. Normally, when you smell body odor on a person, the smell is from their clothes rather than the person. Shower and wash your clothes as much as possible, use deodorant but not as a substitute to washing, use mouthwash but not as a substitute for brushing your teeth. Keep your hair well cut and tidy.

Where possible, always keep a washing or grooming kit handy so when you have time you can freshen up, this will make you feel better as well as sparing other people from smelling you. A simple washing or grooming kit can consist of the following: toothbrush, toothpaste, soap, comb, sewing kit, shoe polish and brushes. If you are working from a hotel towels are always available.

If you have a security room, be it a hotel room or a purpose-built room in a residence, it always needs to be kept clean and tidy. If there are no cleaners, then it will be your job to dust, Hoover, mop and clean the toilets. If you are working a shift system, this needs to be done every time before the next shift takes over. I know you will not have seen a bodyguard with a mop and hover in the movies, but this is reality.

When you are working you will come across many idiots who live in a fantasy world which is a cross between a James Bond film and whatever special forces stories that have been told to them in the pub. This industry attracts this type of person. The mistake a lot of people make is to forget than it is a very small industry and it's easy to check someone out. If you bullshit about your experience, you will be found out.

If you don't know something then ask, don't bluff it. If you are working for a good team they will help you and respect your honesty. If you claim to know everything and done everything people will class you as being full of shit and if there is a problem they will stand back and watch you sort it out. It's easy to test people to see if they are being honest.

Escorts & Formations

The key words to remember when escorting a client on foot are flexibility and adaptability. You must be flexible enough to constantly adapt your formations to the environment you are working in, the threat level, and the manpower available. Whatever formation you are using, it will only be as good as the people you are using in your team. You must select your team carefully. Vet all potential members of your team before you employ them, even if you have known them for a while. A lot of people can talk the business but when they get on operations, they are useless. You should, when time allows, conduct rehearsals of all your team drills so, in the event of an emergency, everyone knows what to do and what everyone else should do.

There are numerous schools of thought on what formations are best. There are advantages and disadvantages to all formations. You must decide which is best for your situation and what you are comfortable working with. When escorting someone, say a celebrity through crowds, it may be necessary to use a tight formation to surround the client with a wall of BGs. If you don't have the personnel to do this, then you will have to consider using an alternative entrance/exit to the venue such as the back door or an obscure fire escape.

Personally, I prefer the use of loose, rather than tight, formations when escorting a client. A lot of people use the US law enforcement statistics on shooting incidents as a base from which to develop their tactics. These statistics are a very valuable source of information but if you look outside the US, you will see that over the past years criminal and terrorist tactics have been changing. The main weapon is the IED. If you do not detect the IED, it will spoil your day no matter what formation you are in.

Since the end of the cold war, there has been an abundance of ex-military weaponry on the Black Market and unemployed former military personnel who are willing to use them or train others to use them. In more and more criminal and terrorist incidents, we are seeing the use of assault weapons, light anti-tank weapons, multiple shooters and military tactics being used. Wherever you are operating, it pays to get to know as much as possible about your opposition and keep up on what other tactics are being used around the world. If you learn the sequence that your opposition will use to attack you, you will be in a better position to predict their moves. The best way to learn how to defend is to learn how to attack.

Body-Cover

The use of body-cover is another debated topic as far as close protection contact drills are concerned. Now, this is where the real-word and Hollywood movies collide on a major scale. The close protection industry attracts those that want a serious professional career and far too many people that wish to re-enforce their masculinity and dream of being heroes.

I have heard too many people state they would take a bullet for their clients, it's their duty... Personally, I would say these people need a mental evaluation and are a risk to their own and others safety. For government employed personnel such as those protecting the Russian, UK or US Presidents etc., sure I understand this as not only are they protecting a person but also national interests. If they are wounded in the line of duty, they will be very well taken care of medically and financially. If they are killed, their families will be compensated and looked after.

This a big difference from the commercial world where if you get hurt, if you're lucky, you might have insurance, if you can't work hopefully you can claim some benefits. If you are seriously injured in an overseas location, hopefully those you are working for have some type of repatriation plan, if not you better have the money yourself.

If you are killed then, who cares, if the story even makes the media you will most probably be labeled a desperado that got what they deserved. Be assured the arm-chair experts will be lining up to give their opinions on how you screwed up just for their two minutes of fame. Hopefully, if you do get screwed up 1. Your client was not a total asshole all the time and 2. You were being well enough paid to compensate for the risk... If you willing to die for $25 an hour I hope the cause worthwhile because the money is not!

Professional Distance

To provide body-cover you have to be close to the client, unlike the movies in reality a lot of clients don't want you next to them, this is where you need to understand professional distance, something which many are clueless about.

Professional distance is the distance you are to be away from the client. Consider this; would you want someone to be within arm's length of you always, listening to your conversations and phone calls etc. This would be annoying and a breach of anyone's privacy and personal security to start with. Most clients want you in sight, but out of earshot, especially if they are with their family, lovers or talking with business partners.

Professional distance is something that can be arranged with a client to what is comfortable with them or with some experience and common sense you can work out for yourself. If all you have ever been taught is to stand next to a client in ridged postures, then your skill set is severely lacking and if you paid to be taught this, you should seek a refund!

Another expectation that always seems to be argued by the tacticool entertainment crowd is that the clients must always have BG in front of them while being escorted. This depends on several factors such as the environment, manpower and if you know where the client is going. Its far more tactically advantageous for small teams to make maximum use of their personnel to dominate the area by using protective surveillance etc. than to rely on the myth of body cover.

Another consideration, bullets penetrate... At the time of writing this I am in South Florida, for my sins... Now, if the local gangbangers are going to do a drive-by or hit, then their weapon of choice is the "Chopper", which is in non-Rap talk is the AK-47. The 7.65X39 round fired by the AK family of weapons will go through 3A concealable vests which, is the choice body armor for most CP personnel and then into whatever is behind them, like a client.

Some will say then you need to wear a plate carrier and higher levels or armor, sure, but you going to look stupid walking around a shopping mall, golf course, chilling in a coffee shop or restaurant while wearing it. Chances are you won't be allowed entry to the previously mention venues and the local security and police will rightfully want to know what the hell you're up to...

People also seem to forget that even if they are wearing plate carriers with armor that will stop a high-velocity round that their vital organs maybe covered but the rest of their bodies are not. Arms, legs and heads are expose and I will let you into a secret... A shot to the head will kill you, shots the arms and legs can immediately disable you, which means you can't defend yourself or escape, and we all know if an artery is severed you can bleed out right... Likewise with the client as the rounds that went into you then go on into them... I have been using 7.62X39 rounds as an example because they are extremely common but 9mm FMJ also have good penetration capabilities against unarmored body parts.

So, with all considerations body cover is more for tacticool entertainment and bar talk than reality, there are far simpler and relevant tactics and techniques that can be employed to ensure the clients safety and more importantly, your safety. But you already know this I am sure....!

Example of an Assassination

An extremist terrorist group decides to assassinate one of their opponents. First, they have to plan when and where to attack the target and assess his security procedures. After several weeks of surveillance, they have discovered that every Tuesday from 14:00 to 16:00, the target visits his sick mother in hospital. The target has four BGs and they always use a four-man box formation. Now the assassins must be selected. The terrorists decide that as well as killing their opponent they will make the assassination a publicity stunt. The terrorists fund and run a school; from here they take two of the best students to have the honor of serving their cause and assassinating their rival. The chosen assassins are two girls in their early teens. The girls receive several hours of training in the use of the AK-47. They are taught to fire controlled bursts from a range of 10 meters into four house doors placed side by side. The four doors represent the area that is taken up by the BGs and the target. After several hours of training the girls, can confidently put 30 rounds in to the doors in a few seconds. The girls also receive some training in the use of cover, what will and will not stop a bullet and just for fun, at the end of their few hours of training; they are shown how to throw a hand grenade.

On the day of the assassination, the girls are shown pictures of the target and his BGs and briefed on their mission. One of the girls is selected to fire first; the other will count to five before opening fire. The girls are dressed in their best clothes and carry their AKs in shopping bags; they are also given a grenade each to be used after they have emptied their AKs. They are taken to the hospital and shown where the best fire positions will be and left to wait for the target to emerge from the hospital. As the target is leaving the hospital at 16:10 with his BGs in their usual box formation, a young girl appears at their 10 O'clock and starts to fire an AK-47 at them. The BGs not hit with the initial bursts of fire react by pulling their client to the ground and drawing their weapons. By this time the second girl at the BGs 2 O'clock has appeared and started to fire at the stationary bodies on the floor. In a matter of 8 seconds, 60 7.62 rounds have been fired at the target and his BGs. In many cases the rounds have gone straight through one BG and in to the client and the other BGs. One of the BGs manages to shoot and kill one of the girls before he passes out from loss of blood. The second girl dies when she pulls the pin on her grenade for it explodes instantaneously.

Immediately the news of the attack is broadcast in the media. The world is outraged at the deaths of the two girls. The terrorist group claims that the girls were part of their youth movement and they were acting on their own initiative. The girls believed their cause was worth the sacrifice. The girls are declared heroes by the terrorists.

There would be several reasons for using the girls to carry out the assassination. Firstly, young girls are not usually suspected of being part of a terrorist organization and can move freely. Secondly, there is the moral issue of whether the BGs will shoot a young girl. A lot of adults would at least hesitate before opening fire-if they opened fire at all. The reason behind the grenade would be to kill the assassin to prevent them from being captured and informing the authorities where they were trained, by whom, and who put them up to the attack. Also, two dead girls make good headlines in the media.

Example Two

We will go straight to where the team are about to leave the hospital. The difference this time is that they are using a different formation. They send an advance man ahead of the formation by a minute or so; the client has two BGs with him in a loose formation and a fourth BG is within shouting distance behind the client and his BGs, watching their backs. As the advance man leaves the hotel, he notices the two girls hanging around but thinks nothing of it. As the client and his BGs leave the hospital, the first girl opens fire on them. The client and the No 1 BG is wounded. The No 2 grabs the client and gets him out of the kill zone. The advance security man alerted by the gunfire turns around and engages and kills the first girl. The BG at the rear of the formation has moved to a flank and is covering the No 2 BG who is moving with the client. The second girl fires a bust from her AK and is engaged and killed by the advance security and rear BG.

A lot of people stress the importance of body cover. This is all well and good in some situations. Any shooter will tell you that it is harder to hit a moving target than a stationary one. If the opposition is using high velocity weapons, the bullets would do straight through you and into the client anyway. Loose formations give you defense in depth and extend you arcs of fire. They also give the BGs a better chance of surviving a contact.

Formations, escorts and contact drills are not something that cannot be taught from a book, they are a practical skill that needs to be practiced and applied. You must be flexible and adapt your tactics and procedures to the environment you are working in.

Protective Surveillance

Protective Surveillance (PS) is a subject that is not taught in a lot of close protection schools. PS, in simple terms, provides the client with covert / undercover protection. For example, we can use covert protection (Protective Surveillance) if the client does not wish others to know that they are or have objects under protection or to protect others without unduly alerting and alarming them to a possible threat. When PS is used in conjunction with the use of regular BG formations it provides the security team with an extra cordon of security.

Going back to the example of the assassination in the last chapter we will look at how things could have turned out if a PS team or person was used. We will start where the client is about to leave the hospital. This time the client is using a three-man team. One BG is to the rear right of the client. There is one man on advance security traveling a minute or so ahead of the client. The third member of the team is on PS. The PS man has been covertly shadowing the client. When the client entered the hospital the PS man took up a position across the road from the hospital at a bus stop. After a while he notices two girls hanging around with odd-shaped shopping bags and he makes a mental note. He receives a call on his mobile phone to alert him that the client is about to leave the hospital. As the client leaves the hospital the PS sees the girls making hasty movements and sees a weapon being pulled from the shopping bags. He shouts a warning to team and engages and kills the first girl. The BG with the client moves him out of the kill zone and back into the hospital. Both the PS and AS have the second girl covered and can engage her, if necessary.

Protective Surveillance

Many supposed professionals in the close protection business don't understand that high profile or low profile visible protection can have negative effects for the client. In the 90's in Eastern Europe after the collapse of the Soviet Union bodyguards would be targeted by criminals providing security services who wanted to take the bodyguard's clients; if the client had just had his protector beaten up in front of him it's in his immediate interests to hire those that had done the beating, right? Visible security personnel can also alert criminals that the client is of some importance, has goods worth stealing or be worth kidnapping. As to those reading this thinking the close protection world is all about being a tough guy, I will tell you you're very wrong, it's about being alert, crafty and cautious.

Also, think about it from a business point of view. If you were going to do business with someone and when you went to meet them they had a bodyguard or two what would you think? Personally, I would be thinking why they needed security, what problems do they have, are those problems going to affect my business dealings with them and possibly put me under threat. Or do they have the security because they don't trust or want to intimidate me. These things need to be taken into consideration when initially putting together options for a client's security program.

There have been times in areas of high organized crime when we have supplied PS personnel who were completely disconnected from the clients, they were providing the clients with a high level of protection but completely untraceable. Communications between the PS team and the clients for itinerary changes etc. went through a 3rd party phone outside of the area of operations. The clients knew the PS team was there as we informed them daily of details of their activities for reassurance. For those who the clients were meeting and doing business with there were no signs they were not trusted, even if they monitored the client's communications nothing would show they had a security team with them.

We have provided protection to numerous clients in sensitive professions without their business associates knowing there was any protection personnel present. One way to do this is to use visual/audio surveillance to monitor the client and place the protection team in an adjoining room or in a close by vehicle. There are many situations where a client cannot have or does not want a bodyguard within arm's reach, this is the real world where the Hollywood and Secret Services techniques do not work!

When PS is used in conjunction with regular close protection/bodyguard details it provides an extra cordon of security. If your client is staying in a hotel or a residence, you could put the building under PS. The PS team would covertly watch the hotel/residence for anyone who is acting suspiciously or watching the hotel. In nearly all assassinations and attacks, the attackers have had their victim under surveillance at some point. It would be the job of the PS to detect any surveillance that would be placed on the client. They would also be dominating any potential surveillance locations by occupying or observing them.

All personnel used for the PS team would have to be surveillance/counter-surveillance trained in addition to being close protection trained. The PS team should be thought of as your early warning system. If it is identified that your client is under surveillance you must up the level of security procedures immediately. This could mean using extra security personnel or getting out of the country that you are in. In addition to upping the client's security, you must act in identifying the people that have your client under surveillance, the PS can undertake this by putting the opposition's surveillance under surveillance.

All PS must be performed covertly, the team must blend in with their environment and not look like BGs. The team members must regularly carry out their counter-surveillance drills, if the PS members are identified by terrorist/criminal surveillance, they will be the first to be killed in the event of an attack on the client. All security team members need to understand that in the event of an attack on the client by semi-professional attackers they would be the first to be targeted. The terrorists/criminals will want to remove the threats to them before they kill or kidnap your client. Also, the threat does not end when your shift ends, organized criminals actively target security personnel and their families. Would you actively protect a client if you knew that if you prevented an attack your family would be killed? As the Narco's say, you can take their silver or their lead!

The PS team should regularly make use of stills cameras and video to survey the people and vehicles that are seen close to the client and in potential surveillance locations. The PS team should study the pictures for any people or vehicles that regularly appear, these people and vehicles could have gone undetected while the PS team was on the ground. For example, if the client went to a restaurant the PS team would video everyone entering and leaving the restaurant while the client was there and just after the client left. They would do the same at the client's next location, the next day etc. If they spot the same people or vehicles at venues while reviewing the videos, it's possible the client is under surveillance. The whole security team would then be made aware of these potential threats and if spotted again they could be put under surveillance by the PS team members.

For the application of protective surveillance by security forces, covert soft target protection tasking's were common in Northern Ireland for the British security forces during the troubles. British security force teams would set up covert Observation Posts (OP) on the houses of off duty military and police personnel living in rural areas or under specific threats. The OP teams tasking was to log and report any activity around the houses, such as who visited, what cars drove past etc. If the same car was spotted driving past the house more times than normal, then the owner and occupants would need to be identified. Also, there were cases where British security forces teams ambushed and killed Irish terrorists while on covert soft target protection tasking's.

Protective surveillance should be employed where resources and manpower are available; on high risk protection details it is essential. Protective surveillance provides you with an early warning of potential threats and if necessary a surprise counter to any attacks upon your team or client.

Advance Security

Advance security is a necessity in all security operations. It can take two forms and may be performed covertly or overtly. It is essential in the planning and operational phases and should be employed whenever the time and manpower are available.

Advance Security in the Planning Phase

When planning an operation, it pays to have someone go to all the locations that you will be visiting in advance. Once there, they will need to make a threat assessment of all the potential threats that might occur and how to avoid them and, if necessary, counter them. If you are going to a foreign country, your advance person or team should make sure that the hotels are suitable, select routes between venues, make first aid arrangements, confirm your communications work, and arrange transportation. These days' videos and photos can be e-mailed back by the advance person or team so the main body of travelers and get a feel for location before they arrive.

Advance Security in the Operational Phase

Advance security in the operational phase of an operation is extremely important and should be employed if you have the necessary manpower, if you are traveling on your own you could possibly hire a local but, will you be able to trust them. If you are traveling in a group you should take turns at being the advance person, if there is a problem it's better to lose only one person rather than the whole group.

The job of the advanced person or team in the operational phase is to proceed you by 10 to 20 minutes and check the route and final location for potential threats and problems. If any threats or problems are detected, the advance person or team will inform you immediately, so that you can go to the secondary plan. For example: We were once working with a client who was going to a potentially hostile South American country, he initially wanted us to supply him with firearms for when he was traveling around the country. But when we made clear the problems that can come with carrying firearms/weapons in a foreign country he began to see the difference between the real world and Hollywood. We organized an advance man for him to arrange his hotel, pick him up from the airport and who would precede him on his travels in a vehicle that fitted in with those being used by the locals. Our operative would inform the client of any problems or anything suspicious along the routes. When he arrived at a location ahead of the client he would check for any threat surveillance personnel etc. Of course, our operative was Latin American in appearance, fluent in Spanish and trained by us.

It is best that all advance work is performed covertly. If a venue or location needs to be checked out, the advance person or team can always claim that they are representing someone else or that they want to hire the venue or stay in the hotel themselves. By performing this duty covertly, they will not give away your itinerary. When performing advance security, wear what helps you to blend in with the environment. There is a fixation in the security and business world that personnel must wear a suit, shirt and tie, this is OK in New York or London but in many countries, you will just stand out from the crowd and make yourself a target. If you look like a business person everyone will think you have money and worth taking the time to rob or kidnap. Always try to dress down and blend in with the people around you.

Staying in a Hotel

It is inevitable that while you are working in our industry that you will spend a lot of time in hotels of some description. Even in a hotel, the client will need static security personnel to look after the rooms when they are not occupied.

This duty involves being sat in a hotel corridor for hours at a time; if you are lucky you will have a hotel room and will be able to sit in the door way and work from there, but you will most probably just have a chair. It is not unusual for personnel to sit in hotel corridors working 12 hours on, 12hours off for weeks at a time. Doing this type of work takes a lot of discipline. You must be clean and well-presented and remain alert at all times. Hotel staff love to tell stories of how they had to wake up some VIP's bodyguard. It happens all the time.

The biggest problem with inexperienced security teams when they are working in hotels is that they think they can do as they like because they are bodyguards. You must remember that you and your client are paying guests in the hotel and can be asked to leave at any time and banned from the hotel. It pays to comply with the hotel rules and procedures and co-operate with the hotel management, security and other staff. In good hotels the staff should be more than willing to help you with any questions or problems you might have.

Many bodyguards look down on hotel staff such as the maids and room service waiters; remember if you need extra toiletries etc. You can get them from the maid so be polite and respectful towards them. If you disrespect the room service waiters, you will never know what is in your food. You want to look upon the hotel staff as an intelligence network. In some cases, the hotel will not be able for legal or other reasons to keep you informed of what other guests are in to the hotel. The maids, porters and room service personnel get to know who is in the hotel and glimpse what baggage they have and what they get up to in their rooms. This is a valuable source of intelligence.

A threat assessment should be compiled on any hotel that you are planning to stay in and orders written for the stay. Whether your client is staying for a day or a week, you will need to speak to the hotel management and security and work out plans for your stay that are acceptable to the hotel and will not hinder your operational procedures. You should leave the contact phone numbers for your security personnel with the hotel staff, so they can contact you direct in the case of any problems. Where possible the security team should be in place before the client arrives. All rooms being used by the client need to be searched for IEDs, bugs and other suspicious objects. A routine needs to be established for the corridor security and they must be briefed on the limit of their responsibility and how they should challenge anyone coming in to that area. If possible, the client's rooms should be above the second story and not looked into by other buildings.

The best position for the room is at the end of a corridor; if the client has taken a few rooms in the middle a corridor it will cause you problems with other guests passing in front of your client's door when coming and going to their rooms. The corridor security team should have the details of all other security personnel working with the client. They will also need the details and of all the other staff who are traveling with the client. If the client has many staff, it is advisable that photos of the staff should be with their details to help with identification. In addition, they will need a list of all cars that are being used. All these details should be kept in a logbook with all other useful phone numbers.

If the security team has a room to work from, then this should be used as a control room. Maps for the area should be placed on boards/team laptop/pad and all locations and routes used by the client marked as well as all hospitals, police stations, safe houses and emergency rendezvous points etc. Copies of the orders and threat assessment should also be kept on with the logbooks. Before any non-member of the security team enters the room the map boards, laptops and any log books need to be put away so they cannot see the details of the operation. No one from outside of the client's staff should be let into any of the client's rooms unattended. Also confirm which members of the staff are allowed unattended into the client's personal rooms.

Every time the client returns to the hotel, the clients BG should inform the corridor security personnel 15 to 12 minutes before their arrival. Where manpower allows, this gives the corridor security personnel time to check the hotel lobby and entrance etc. for anything or anyone suspicious. If anything, suspicious is spotted, the client's BG must be informed immediately. A logbook needs to be kept for all the comings and goings from the client's rooms. The client's staff should be booked in and out of their rooms by the corridor security. Details of when the client leaves the hotel, with whom, in what vehicle and were they are going needs to be logged down. If done properly, the corridor security personnel on duty should know where everyone involved with the operation is at all times and be able to contact them.

Considerations for a hotel stay:
- Complete a threat assessment on the hotel before your stay.
- Compile a set of orders for the duration of the stay in the hotel.
- Liaison and co-operate with hotel staff.
- Try to check out other guests.

- Regularly check all public area of the hotel.
- The client's rooms should be above the second floor and at the end of a corridor.
- Will you put the hotel under protective surveillance?
- Check that the hotel is not under surveillance from other agencies/criminals.
- Search all rooms before occupation.
- Let no one into the rooms from outside of the client's party unattended.
- Check the hotel for communications dead spots.
- Vet hotel staff where possible.
- Room keys need to be controlled by corridor security team. Remember the hotel staff has masters.
- The use of the room phones by the client's staff needs to be controlled.
- Who, from the client staff, is not allowed alcohol?
- Who is paying the hotel bills?
- What is the budget on ordering food from room service?
- Luggage needs to be booked in item by item and never left unattended.
- Try to blend in with the environment.
- What CCTV does the hotel have?
- Will the hotel let you put up your own cameras in the corridors?
- The corridor security team should be informed of any deliveries for the client's rooms.
- Keep a check on who is having food etc. from room service. It is a fraud for drivers etc. to order food when not entitled to it and signs in someone else's name.

Attending Events

The reason for a lot of duties is to attend corporate events and social functions with clients, these can prove to be troublesome, if not planned properly. Most function venues will have their own security personnel and procedures, the standard of these can range from very good to accidents simply waiting to happen. I know of one very high-profile hotel in London that had all their banqueting furniture stolen by a group of men claiming they were there to pick the furniture up for cleaning, they loaded it all up into a truck in broad daylight and were never seen again.

Over the years I have provided security for a wide range of corporate events, meetings, social functions and encountered problems ranging from flooding, permitting issues, paparazzi, assaults, drug use and prostitution. As with hotels, most event organizers do not put a high priority on security and usually, at most may hire a guard or two to stand at the main entrance. I have worked VIP functions where Politicians and Royalty have been present by myself because the event organizers did not book more security personnel, at these events there was no way for one person to secure the venue. Luckily, nothing went wrong but I never understand why people will spend tens of thousands of dollars on organizing a function and consider security as an unnecessary expense. I am sure many of those attending such events expect a decent standard of security and would be concerned if they knew the real story.

One weak spot I have repeatedly seen, internationally, is that temporary staff are rarely profiled, vetted and in many cases are undocumented workers. A lot of large venues use temp agencies to supply them with dish washers, waiters and bar staff for functions; they do not keep such people on staff as they do not need them all the time. You can have metal detectors at the main entrance of a venue, every guest searched, every door in the venue manned by a trained and competent security person, but the chances are none of the regular and temp venue staff will be searched and they are the ones that will be serving food, drinks, manning bag and coat checks.

As with everything else, do your threat assessment and do not trust others to have your security at the top of their priority list. Here is a list of things that you need to take into consideration when attending events.

Considerations for Attending an Event

- Compile a threat assessment on the venue and consider who attending may have an active threat on them.
- Get the full postal address, contact numbers and a map grid number for the venue. Look on Google earth and assess the venue and the surrounding area.
- Consider if there are any building's around or on routes approaching the venue that could be targets for criminals or terrorists.
- Do you have the name and number of a contact person at the venue or with the event organizers who can answer any questions you might have?
- If possible send an advance person to check out the venue and the surrounding area, remind them to take plenty of photos and video of the layout of the place
- Examine, in detail, the layout of the building and note all: entrance and exit points, stairwells, elevators, escape routes and potential safe rooms.
- Will the venue have been searched for explosive devices and weapons, if yes, by whom and what security procedures have been put in since the search?
- What time will you arrive and is there a cut off time for entrance?
- How will you get to the venue, if you are driving where will you park and is the area secure?
- If invitations or tickets are required will they need to be shown on entry; who will responsible for looking after the invitations and tickets?
- If reservations or tickets need to be booked try not to use your name, use a company or cover name.
- What entrances will you use, what security is there, will you be searched and are those conducting the searches competent?
- Will you or anyone else be able to take weapons into the venue?
- What alternative entrances and exits are there, such as fire exits or those marked for staff?
- Give all entrances and exits code numbers so that if you need to evacuate you can communicate with your group or driver without anyone else knowing which exit and route you're using?
- If using a driver where will they be parked and how long will it take them to get to each exit, make sure they know the codes numbers for the exits.
- What facilities are there for drivers; food, drink and toilets etc.
- What facilities are there at or close to the venue; pay phones, bathrooms, restaurants, hotels, stores etc.
- What is the overall program for the event and what is your program.

- Where will you be seated, is a good position that has a good view of the venue and is close to exits?
- Do any other guests have threats on them, if yes, where will they be seated?
- Will you be dining and who will prepare the food?
- Do you or anyone one in your group have any special dietary requirements?
- If you are using bodyguards where will they be located and what, if any, are the dinning arrangements for them?
- Will media or photographers be present and what restrictions will be placed on them?
- Will security or police personnel be present, and will they be armed?
- Will security and police personnel be in uniform or plain clothes, if plain clothes will they be wearing any form of identification?
- Will guests and staff wear identification badges? Try to see or get examples of all types of identification so you can hopefully verify a fake from a real one.
- Will your communications work in the venue, what alternatives are there?
- What first aid facilities are available, where is the nearest hospital with an emergency room and what are the best routes to get there?
- What firefighting equipment is there at the venue, where is it located and is it serviceable?
- What are the response times for the emergency services for incidents ranging from a guest having a heart attack to a terrorist attack?
- Make plans and procedures for how you're going to react to all the threats you have identified in your threat assessment be it food poisoning or a terrorist attack.
- Make sure you know how to raise the alarm in the case of an emergency or anti-social behaviour such as drug use or drunkenness etc.
- Find out what the venue's official evacuation procedures are and then make your own; in the case of a terrorist attack the terrorists would most probably know the official evacuation procedures and would have booby trapped or ambushed these exits and routes out of the venue.
- Plan escape routes to exits form all areas of the venue.
- Have code words within your group for emergencies as you do not want others to know what you're doing or where you're going.
- Is there a suitable location that could be used as a safe room and how long could you hold out there for?
- Allocate emergency rendezvous points outside of the venue and make sure everyone in you group knows them. These are important because if you group is separated during an evacuation you can quickly re-group again. Also, if you're using a driver and there is an emergency at the venue they may not be able to get close to pick you up due to traffic or a police cordon. It may be easier for you to walk a couple of blocks away from the venue where it would be less congested.

- Plan primary and secondary routes to your residence and safe houses from the venue.

You can see from this list that going to business and social functions can take some thinking about. As I stated in a previous most people are unaware of what is going on around them and when there is an emergency are clueless on how to react. You don't want to be one of these people and it does not take much effort not to be!

Attending Meetings

Meetings can be extremely dangerous and should always be treated with caution, this is where people will know where you will be at specific time, just what the bad guys want to know. Arranging meetings is an easy way to set someone up for kidnapping, assassination, sexual assault or robbery.

Meetings should be kept as secret as possible and planned well in advance, when under a high threat you want to exchange the maximum amount of information with those you are meeting with in the shortest possible time.

Firstly, you will need to select a suitable meeting location, be it a coffee shop or a hotel suite, this will depend on how many people you'll be meeting with, what's to be discussed and what is the threat level. You should always have a reason and cover story for being in that area at that time in case the meeting is compromise; for example, maybe you or those you are meeting with have identified they are under active surveillance.

Everyone involved in the meeting will need a covert way of alerting the others that they have been followed or are under active surveillance. This can be done by using codes or signs en-route to the meeting location or quickly posted comments on online chat boards or social media sites. This way if one person is compromised they should not compromise or endanger those they are meeting with. Cell phones should not be used or taken to sensitive meetings as they can be tracked and used as listening devices, they should also not be used to warn others that you are under surveillance, calls and text messages would lead straight to those you were meeting with. A low-tech method such you drinking soda instead of coffee or putting the do not disturb sign is on the hotel suite door could tell the person your meeting with that things have gone bad.

Whenever you are meeting people for the first time you should always use prearranged signs and counter signs to confirm their identity. The simplest thing is a pre-arranged question and answer, this works better than checking ID cards as the person your meeting with might be the right person, but you know them by a pseudonym. In a basic context you want to make sure the limo driver who is meeting you at the airport is your real driver and will take you to your hotel not into months of captivity or to a garbage dump!

Theory Put into Practice

I spoke with Jerry Arrechea a corporate security manager and world champion martial artist based in Mexico City. Mexico has one of the highest crime rates in the world and is second only to Syria for its murder and violent death rates, so I wanted to know what Jerry recommends to his clients for keeping themselves safe.

In Mexico we must deal with a wide array of security problems ranging from drug cartel violence to general street crime and there is no magic solution. The criminals here are professional, they plan and organize their crimes from the initial surveillance of their targets to how to escape after the crimes have been committed. It's important for us to be able to identify the criminals in the surveillance and planning stage of their operations and take counter measures. The last thing we want is a confrontation as the criminals are usually very well armed and not afraid to shoot, we would sooner lose goods or money than put our clients in hostile situations.

One situation where we are always extra carful is when we are attending meetings in unfamiliar areas especially with people we don't know 100% as these meetings could be set ups for robberies or kidnappings. Before the meeting we do a thorough due diligence check on those we are meeting with, on the day of the meeting we sweep the area looking for anyone or vehicles that look suspicion and usually employ protective surveillance personnel while the meeting is taking place to alert us of any suspicious activity that may take place in the area. I advise all my clients, especially females to be cautious when attending meetings where they will be isolated even if they are meeting with people they know to some degree. I have a female self-defense client who is a luxury real estate agent and has had several issues with clients over the years who have tried to sexually assault her while she is showing properties. These days she always has a male driver take her to appointments, has worked out a plan of action if she is attacked and always has something close at hand she can use as a weapon. The last wannabe playboy, someone who she had met before, that tried to touch her inappropriately ended up with two broken fingers and a broken nose, all her driver had to do when he came to her assistance was throw the now whimpering playboy off the property....

This lady's driver is a well-trained and dedicated guy, but it still took him time after being alerted to get to her location. She feels it can be intimidating for her clients if she had a bodyguard shadowing her, so her driver usually waits in the car. This why she had worked out her immediate reaction drill as she knew it would take 15 to 45 seconds for her driver to get to her assistance. Everyone should think about how they would react to an assault and put a plan in place. Even if you are in an area where the police will come quickly to your assistance, you must know how to alert them you're in danger and then protect yourself until they are able to get to you. As I said earlier, there is no magic fix, you must be aware of your environment and have plans in place for how to avoid potentially hostile situations and in the worst-case scenarios how to use force to defend yourself!

Considerations for Attending Meetings

- Do you know in detail the meeting location? If not, then check it or get someone trusted to check it.
- Things to take into consideration include the facilities (bathrooms, cafes, taxis, payphones etc.), potential surveillance positions, location of surveillance cameras, escape routes
- Will it be daylight or dark?
- What is the condition of pedestrian and vehicle traffic, what are people wearing, age and type of people in the area?
- Make plans and procedures for all possible emergencies identified in your threat assessment.
- Consider where along your route to the meeting location you would put surveillance personnel to watch you if you were the opposition and identify where on your approach to the meeting location you would be channeled.
- How will you get to the meeting location walking, using public transport or driving?
- If driving where will you park your car, will it be secure or hidden, how long would it take you to get back to it in an emergency and what are you going to do if it's compromised?
- What will you wear for the meeting and will you need a change of clothes, remember it's always easier to dress down than up. You can always take off a sports coat and shirt and put them in a plastic bag.
- Will you be carrying any weapons and is there any risk of being searched?
- Always be aware of what's going on in the environment around you; watch for warning signs posted by the those your meeting with that could indicate they have been compromised, any unusual activity, people waiting in cars or vans with blacked out windows, fit young men with short hair hanging around for no reason, read the body language of those waiting in possible surveillance positions etc.
- When you reach the meeting, location sweep the area for anything suspicious, you might not be under surveillance but the person your meeting with could be.
- If you can, select good position at the meeting location from where you can view as many entrances as possible, be close to escape routes and view what's going on the street outside without being in clear view from outside.
- Locate those you are meeting with and exchange passwords, consider walking them to another location to identify if they are under surveillance.
- If you are going to eat and drink, consider the method of payment; credit cards leave a paper trail.
- Also, do not leave your food or drink unattended or let anyone fetch you a drink from the bar etc. As this is an opportunity to drug it.

- Under a high threat make sure you do not leave anything behind from which finger prints or a DNA sample could be taken from.
- During the meeting constantly watch for physical, video and audio surveillance, if you have the manpower get a trusted associate to do this for you and to watch your back.
- Keep the meeting as short as possible and when it's is over leaving the area as quickly as possible and conduct several counter surveillance drills, consider changing your appearance if necessary.
- If further meetings are required, they would have to be varied for different times of day and days of the week.

Close Protection & Personal Security in Hostile Crowds

Over the years I have been caught up in several situations with crowds where things could have gone very bad, very quickly. Crowds are best avoided at all cost when providing close protection/bodyguard services, but some clients' want, or need be at the center of the party or in the thick of the action, and they are paying the bills!

Two good examples of why crowds should be avoided are the incidents that happened in 1998 in Northern Ireland to British Army Corporals Derek Wood and David Howes and the attack on the CBS journalist Lara Logan in Tahrir Square, Egypt in 2011. Research and study these incidents and use them for brain storming prior to your operational planning to ensure you don't make the same mistakes. It's easy to criticize other people's actions from a distance; we want to learn not criticize.

Corporals killings: https://en.wikipedia.org/wiki/Corporals_killings
Lara Logan: https://en.wikipedia.org/wiki/Lara_Logan

In 1988 in Northern Ireland two off-duty plan cloths soldiers, Corporals Derek Wood and David Howes drove into the funeral procession for a IRA terrorist. Why they were there we will never know, the theory is they were lost and came off a designated route or were site seeing. They were trapped by the crowd, dragged from their car and executed with their own firearms.

I am sure many of you are asking yourselves why they did not shoot their attackers. To start with these were not Infantry soldiers but signalers, also the rules of engagement in Northern Ireland were extremely strict. I am sure if they started to shoot their unarmed attackers and survived the situation they would still be in jail on murder charges. The terrorist's lawyers would be screaming human rights violations with their media and American friends calling it an unjustified massacre. No win situation right so, avoid crowds!

So, if they took aggressive action they would have to deal with the legal consequences, plans for the aftermath of a use of force incident need to always be in place. At that time in Northern Ireland off duty troops only carried 10 rounds for their pistols, so would they have had enough ammunition to get out of the situation to start with?

This second incident from Tahrir Square, Egypt in 2011 is where the CBS journalist Lara Logan was dragged into a crowd and sexually assaulted. I have worked with news crews and understand that a lot of times they need to take a risk to get the story they are after. This is where the worst-case scenario should always be assessed and prepared for. From a close protection point of view, the clients need to be made aware of the threats, even if the ignore the warning (KYA).

Rule 1. The streets can go very bad, very quickly, wherever you are! What can we learn from this incident and what could have been done differently? I think it's clear their security man did everything he physically could possible but one man against a 100 has no chance, and in close quarters he was lucky not to be seriously injured, stabbed or killed himself. Many of these news agencies policy's is that they don't use armed security and he could not have legally had a firearm there anyway. Non-lethal or improvised maybe, pepper spray might have been an option, but I doubt it would be available or legal. You also need to consider if your use of force will escalate the situation, a lot to consider right!

I have written about this many times before, just because someone is big and calls themselves a security guard, bodyguard etc. does not mean they know what they are doing or will risk getting hurt protecting you! I expect the two local guards the news crew's fixer arranged were just big friends of his who wanted to earn a few dollars, so I don't blame them for disappearing then things went bad.

When things started to go bad they needed to get to their vehicles ASAP but I take it the evacuation route to the vehicles was blocked and the vehicles were too far away. I had this happen to me once before in bad part of Haiti due to the clients heading in one direction and the local drivers heading in the other... The drivers had more common sense than the clients...

One thing that could have been done would have been to hire a couple of local police or military personnel, well ask for a favor... But if this could have been done would be down to budget and the news agencies policies on working with police etc. as they are generally trying to stay neutral in a situation.

Hopefully this article with give you a few things to think about and in a perfect world it's best to avoid crowds, but in reality, it's nearly impossible. I have given two extreme examples here that you should research but, be it a sports event, street carnival or political event remember rule 1. The streets can go very bad, very quickly!

Killing with Kindness

*The devil does not come to you with a red face and horns,
he comes to you disguised as everything you ever wanted!*

When going over threat assessments with security consultants, executive protection personnel and the like it amazes me that the vast majority of people only consider and plan for dealing with the threats of physical violence or theft. Their operational plans then usually consist of nothing more than supplying as many armed personnel, armored cars and house alarms as the budget will allow. Providing your clients with a serious security program, in my opinion, would mean you have to be pro-active and preventative, not reactive.

To start with, what people forget is that in most countries it is impossible for foreigners to legally carry firearms for self-defense and if locals can carry firearms the laws on use of force are usually very strict; obtaining the weapons and permits can be very difficult and expensive. More importantly while armed guards, trained or untrained, can reassure a client and deter your basic street criminal, for the professional criminals they are just a show that presents little danger.

I tell my clients that I place the threat from blackmail and kidnapping a lot higher than that of assassination. Think about it, if someone is executed what use are they, none... But if someone can be entrapped, blackmailed and manipulated they can provide the criminals with an ongoing source of funds or information etc. If someone is kidnapped, they are a valuable asset which can be ransomed or used as a barging tool to influence the decisions of others.

Now, think like a criminal who is going to kidnap someone who is traveling with armed bodyguards, would you want to get into a shootout with the bodyguards and risk your life, that of the person you want to kidnap and alert the police or military, or would you rather do things more discreetly.

Organized criminals and drug cartel members are business people, they are out to make money, so how will killing people make them money. In some of the emerging markets assassination is the unofficial way of solving business disputes as assassins are usually a lot cheaper to hire than lawyers. A person is usually assassinated to be removed from the equation or to be made an example of; most people should never be faced with the threat of targeted assassination.

"Plata o Plomo" (Silver or Lead) is a common criminal saying in Latin America and it means take my money or take my bullets. This is not just a Latin American phenomenon, in the late 90's I had dealings with a guy in Eastern Europe who was tactically and self-defense wise very capable. He was working for a state police unit protecting a politician, who had, let's say, had Mafia issues, as most people with any influence did in those days. The Mafia group's initial approach to the politician was not directly to him; they first contacted the wives of the bodyguards on his security detail. And, as usual the initial approach was very polite and offering financial rewards for favors... So, who's more important to you, a client or your family?

In the real-world fighting is for amateurs; think about it from the criminal's point of view, there are many ways to make a protection team operationally ineffective and the use of force is nowhere near the top of this list. To start with, most people's standard of personal security is extremely low. They're a bodyguard and have a gun right, people are scared of them, right? Well, maybe their reflection in the mirror when they are taking selfies in the bathroom wearing their best suit and tie is...

If you can't protect yourself how can you protect others? Professional personal security is 24/7, not just for the length of a detail or shift. From a commercial point of view, you certainly need to promote yourself but that does not mean letting everyone at Starbucks hear your work-related conversations or look over your shoulder to see who you're chatting with online. I should not have to mention to you the need to be careful what you post on social media, but...

In most places in the world drugs are freely available, so why should a criminal need to get into a shootout when they can just drug their target's security team. It's common for people to get drugged in bars and clubs for robbery or rape but many professionals in the security business don't consider this threat to security details. What would it take for a server at your regular coffee shop to spike your morning latte with Ketamine, GHB or Rohypnol? I am sure if your threat comes from semiprofessional criminals they will be assessing your routine, and I am sure the barista who is making your morning coffee with a smile will happily take the criminals silver rather than lead. A basic Gypsy robbery tactic in Europe is to get their small children to go out and sell glasses of tea or soft drinks to tourists. Would you expect a little girl to give you a spiked drink?

Always know where your food and drink is coming from, always be suspicious of gifts and never leave food or beverages unattended in public or with strangers, especially attractive women you have just met. The common date rape drugs like Rohypnol, GHB, Ketamine are tasteless and odorless, take approximately 15 to 30 minutes to take effect and usually last three to six hours, depending on dosage. These drugs make the victims weak, unconscious and unable to remember what happened. Prescription drugs such as Klonopin and Xanax have similar effects especially in large doses.

A drug that is regularly used in crimes in Colombia, Venezuela and Ecuador is Burandanga or Scopolamine which is extracted from the Borrachero tree. Scopolamine has numerous legitimate medical uses but when used by rapists and criminals it renders their victims into a compliant zombie-like state of which they remember nothing. Victims have the outward appearance of being okay but are in fact in a trance and are totally unaware of what they're doing. Victims of Scopolamine overdoes are common in Colombian hospitals as are the deaths of those who received a large dose or had a low tolerance. This drug is more common that people think. I have come across similar ones in Haiti and West Africa; once administered through liquid or powder form the victim is completely compliant and helpless.

In the late 90's in Eastern Europe I knew of one very low-profile government agency that suffered several fatalities from targeted chemical attacks. The initial killings were not recognized as targeted assassination as the victims had died in car crashes. What sparked concern was that during the autopsies the victims who were otherwise fit and in good physical conditions had fluid in their lungs. They had been killed by an anesthesia drug placed in the ventilation intake of their cars, so when they were running the car's heating system the anesthesia was dispersed inside the car and they died from a chemical overdose combined and covered with a car crash.

In 2002 Russian special forces used an anesthesia drug to end the hostage crisis at Nord-Ost Theater in Moscow. The drug, Kolokol-1, was pumped into the theater through the ventilation/heating system and knocked out everyone inside, all the terrorists were killed but unfortunately so were 130 of the hostages, reportedly due to adverse effects from the drug. A much lower tech version of this would be to spray pepper or OC spray into a building's ventilation intake, the gas would disperse throughout the building and affect anyone inside if sufficient quantities were used.

One of the best and most effective weapons organized criminals have and use is sex. I remember as a 17-year-old British infantryman first in basic training and then Northern Ireland being warned that the Irish Terrorists used to send women into the bars to pick up (honey trap) soldiers; when the troops went home with these young ladies instead of getting sexual favors they got a beating or a bullet in the head from the girls waiting accomplices.

The tactic of the "honey trap" is where, let's say a female will approach and start a conversation with a male, who may be a pre-planned target or just someone who looks like he has money. The aim of the female is to get the male to go with her to a hotel room or apartment for sex. If the male goes with her then the trap can develop in several ways. A crude honey trap would be where the male is drugged or beaten and then robbed. A more intricate honey trap would involve the man being videoed having sex with the female, the more deviant the better, and then blackmailed for favors or hard currency.

Think about it, how many guys do you know who would say NO if you gave them a gift of an afternoon in a decent hotel room with two attractive young ladies who were there to please? Now, I am sure most security professionals would say they would never do such things while on a detail or in life in general, but I will say they are talking Bullshit. Boys will be Boys, I understand this and know that some men when away from their wives, families and regular environments will take every opportunity to party.

I once got a short-term job in a conservative Middle Eastern country for someone I work on the circuit with in London. He is former British army and had a good career in the British Police. He has an accomplished background and also an addiction to Tinder, which I thought would have been blocked in the country we were in. When not working he was doing his best to meet up with and try to sleep with any woman that would have him, even though unmarried couples caught having relations in that country would lead to both parties being thrown in jail. In this situation the only person he was a danger to was himself and to be honest if he had gotten himself arrested apart from it being highly amusing for me it would have been a good introduction to the real world for him after his career in the sheltered environments of the British military and police.

So, from a management point of view you need to ensure your people are experienced and mature enough not to be tempted by any woman that looks in their direction. In Eastern Europe it's not uncommon to get prostitutes phoning your hotel room offering their services; your details supplied by their associates working in the hotel. Would you say no, would the people you're working with say no?

Whether prostitutes are found online, at a strip bar or supplied by other sources they can all bring big problems, not only disease but also robbery and blackmail. The U.S. secret service had major issues in 2012 in Cartagena, Colombia. The agents were stupid enough to take prostitutes they met in a night club to their hotel rooms where they had their weapons, presidential security plans, phones and computers etc. There are plenty of "by the hour" hotels in Colombia, so why take a hooker to your hotel? The less your new friend knows about you the better, even if you are in love!

Their behavior can only be described as completely stupid and the whole affair came to light after they refused to pay a girl her agreed fee and she called the cops on them. In many places the police provide security and act as enforces for sex workers, they earn some extra money or favors in return. Maybe in this case the secret service agents would have been better off in the short term if the girl's protectors were Cartel and not local police, but in the long-term favors would have needed to be returned, nothing is ever free!

Again, asking from a management point of view: would a security detail for a senior Cartel member be put in the same situation as the secret service agents? I think not. I am sure, if required they would have access to trusted women in a neutral location. I am also sure that if they committed the same security negligence as the secret service agents they would be lucky to just get a bullet in the head.

Five Star hotels and exclusive venues are always a favored hangout for attractive women seeking to better themselves and make some hard currency in the process. Be it London, Paris, Miami or Port Harcourt these ladies will not be hard to find. One funny story, that could have led to big problems, involves a gentleman I know who exchanged phone numbers with a very attractive lady he met in a high-end hotel lobby in West Africa. After an evening exchanging texts, he invited the girl to his hotel room. When she got there an argument quickly broke out as he did not realize he had to pay for her time, I think his ego was hurt. He ended up, when the situation was made clear to him, paying the girl, which was the right thing to do. He was dumb and had wasted her time, for her it was business, if he just wanted a conversation he should have Skyped his wife.

A lot of the sex business is run by organized crime and in a lot of places as I have said the police provide protection for the venues and the girls. The criminals and police also use the girls to provide them with intelligence on potential targets for blackmail, extortion or kidnapping. With a call to her friends in the police our dumb friend's actions in West Africa could have caused him and maybe the rest of the security team a lot of third world problems which would have cost everyone a lot more than the girl's fee to make go away.

Now think about this scenario, you're in your hotel room in a developing country and there is a knock on your door. When you answer it there is the hotel manager and two police officers who ask to search your room, are you going to say no, can you say no? When they look under your bed they find an illegal handgun, hopefully they give you an option to pay a fine and not just drag you off to a 3rd world prison? Do you think anyone will believe the gun was not yours; there are 3 witnesses who were present when it was found. So, how could an illegal weapon, drugs or child porn end up in your hotel room or residence. Well maybe via any attractive young ladies your team has decided to entertain or if you're married you could always blame the hotel staff.

Think about what you would do in your own country if your car was broken into or you come home one day to find your front door has been forced open. Call the cops? Most people would wait for the cops to turn up and then make entry to the house or let the cops check for finger prints etc. But what's going to happen if the cops enter your house and find illegal drugs or look under your car seat and find a firearm, that hopefully for your sake has not been used in a crime. In some obvious break-ins you need to be more concerned about things being put in place rather than what's been taken!

In many places the police, judges and legal system are for hire and at the service of the highest bidder or the best connected. One good example of this was highlighted to me when I was offered a security job in a fairly remote part of Eastern Europe, again in the late 1990's, for clients who had dispute with a local governor over some very valuable assets. At the time I had very good contacts in the country who made it very clear to me there was no way to provide security in that region.

We could hire the most capable people in that area but even though they would be working for us they were answering to that region's governor. Their families, their jobs and their whole lives were there. Would they risk all of this for a short-term contact? I know they wouldn't! It was in their best interest to take our money but also to inform on us and work against our interests.

So, why not take in a security detail from another area, well we did not think it would take long before they were arrested for some reason. Again, the governor controlled the region which meant the police, courts and judges. There would be no need for Hollywood shootouts, the whole security detail could be arrested by a superior number of well-armed police on trumped up weapons, drugs charges etc. I am sure after a few days of being abused in prison and media headlines declaring the illegal activities of these guns for hire the judge would do his duty and give them a long custodial sentence. This would also highlight to the client that it would be in his interests to just comply with the governor's wishes and live happy ever after.

So, hopefully you can see from this short chapter there are a lot of real threats out there that need to be taken into consideration when working a security detail, more than just the threat of physical assault. A lot of the issues I have highlighted here can occur in Western Europe and the U.S., you don't have to be in one of today's high-risk countries. If your threat assessment identifies a threat from serious criminals you need to consider and plan for all possible threats, put yourself in the criminal's shoes and think how you would target yourself. Always remember, if you can't solve a problem with money, then you can always solve it with a lot of money... Let's just hope you have the money...

The Sex Business

It always surprises me how many guys especially those in the security industry don't understand the sex business and end up in trouble because they get duped by girls using routines that have been around since women realized how dumb guys were. Looking back, I was very lucky at being exposed the realities of the sex business in my late teens while serving in the British Army in Cyprus. I was in an Infantry unit and after a two-year tour of Northern Ireland we were posted to the Mediterranean Island for two years, which with its abundance of cabaret clubs proved to be a very good training ground for an inquisitive 19-year-old squaddie.

Like in most places the cabaret clubs and prostitution business in Cyprus is a Mafia run business, at the time the working girls were from mainly Asian with some Eastern Europe's. Were they the victims of sex trafficking; I am sure they were making more money as hookers in Cyprus than they would in their own countries, business is business. To be honest I never heard of our guys being scammed by the girls, but we were just young soldiers with little to offer and nothing to lose. For most of us the novelty quickly wore off as the abundance of tourists meant getting laid was not a problem and the polite girls even paid for the drinks.

But, boys will be boys and we had those that fell in love with these working girls. As I remember several of the guys who were spotted much too regularly in the cabarets and even went to the Philippines Embassy in Nicosia to try to help the girls get a ticket home. I am sure the girls were just playing the sympathy card for some extra cash or hoping these naïve young men with British Passports would marry them and give them access to the European Union. I bet if the girls knew what the guys whose virginity they took were doing to help them they would not have been very happy. I am sure they really wanted to be deported back to where they come from and explain to the businessmen who arranged their flights, visas and employment how they were going to pay their debt off.

It's a fact of life that people have vices and I do not judge people on what they do in private, as long as it is between consenting adults. I discuss the sex business with my clients as it's an area where unwary people can and do get themselves into a lot of trouble. One example of an avoidable problem was the situation the U.S. Secret Service had in Cartagena, Colombia, which was absolutely ridiculous on many levels. Recently the charities Oxfam and the Red Cross have had employees accused of sex abuse and I think it's a common accusation against United Nations troops.

The most common and accepted side of the sex industry are the strip bars and they can be found in most places, some are very classy and well-run businesses, but many are not. During the late 90's I had more than a few business meetings in strip clubs in central, eastern Europe and also supplied security for several clubs in London, so I know a little bit about how things work. You need to understand this basic fact; more than most places as soon as you walk through the door you are a commodity.

The sex business is a business, it's all about hard currency, so forget the emotions. Remember you're paying for the show, you're paying for attention and the working girls are just doing their job as long as you're paying. Strips bars should be thought of as the same way you think about a patisserie. You go, select your cake, buy it, enjoy it and move on until next time. Many times, in Europe I have seen the drunk businessman trying to dance while surrounded by two or three hot young women; if he has the money and he wants them they are his, for a few hours or the night at least.

Hopefully before the gentleman leaves the club either alone or with the girl who's within his price range, he has avoided some of the common issues with strip bars and clip joints. A typical scam is to vastly overcharge for drinks, when the bill is presented our gent finds out his couple of beers cost a few hundred dollars. When he protests he is confronted by a couple of thugs who shows him the price list for drinks, which is well-hidden behind the bar. In most cases he will have his wallet emptied and may be escorted to an ATM machine and instructed to draw out more money or just beaten and robbed. If the gentleman is with friends, one may be held in the venue while the other is sent to get more money. These operations rely on the fact that the people going into these places will not report these incidents to the police as they don't want people, such as their wives and bosses to know that they were in a sleazy strip bar in the first place.

It was common in Eastern Europe for those who flashed money and jewelry around in the clubs to end up drugged and robbed, their drinks being spiked by the bar staff or those they were socializing with. If they reported the robberies to the police they would not be taken seriously, what was to prove they did not drink themselves unconscious, they could not remember what they were doing, so they could have given their valuables away etc.

The threat from violence is also always present, be it from the jealous guy who's infatuated with the girl that's giving you all the attention tonight or the wannabe gangster that see's you as an easy source of a few dollars. Most of the working girls are also more than capable of hurting more than your feelings, don't be surprised if the pretty young thing who took your wallet defends her honor by putting a glass in your face; now explain that to your wife after the bouncer's finish throwing you out.

In most places prostitution is illegal but, in some places, it is a licensed business and even where it's illegal, you will not have to look far to find sex for sale. In Eastern Europe it's not uncommon to get hookers phoning your hotel room offering their services; your details supplied by their associates working in the hotel. Or the hotel concierge can arrange girls for you, maybe for a fee but be assured everyone is making a percentage of any deals that the prostitutes makes with you.

Whether the hookers are found online, at a strip bar or supplied by other sources they can all bring big problems, not only disease but also robbery and blackmail. If the hooker has friends in the hotel they can access your hotel registration details, which will more than likely include your home address, business address and credit card details. How much would most men pay to stop the photos or video from their hotels security cameras showing him and a young lady getting cozy in the hotel bar and then going to his room being sent to his wife? Get the picture?

I have heard quite a few stories of men taking hookers to their business and their homes when their families are not there because they are too cheap to get a hotel room, I usually hear the stories when they start to be extorted.

While providing security for high-end events in London's West End I have had numerous arguments with very well dressed, attractive young ladies trying to gatecrash exclusive events. At one very stuffy black-tie event two stunning girls managed to bypass security by paying the £500.00 each for tickets and at the rate they were giving out business cards I am sure they made a profit on their investment that night alone.

For the high-end and well-connected girls when not socializing or on call in exclusive venues, they tend to work from apartments in usually very nice parts of town. And for those that can afford them they are a far safer bet than the girls that you will encounter at the strip bars. For the starting fee of $1000.00 for an evening of conversation with the option to negotiate for sexual favors you should also secure maximum discretion. But be assured the girls and their employers have taken their precautions, these days usually in the form of their apartments being equipped with covet cameras which are monitored by a close at hand minder. An incriminating video is a lot harder to explain away than a few cuts and bruises, right?

But I am sure most of these city gents and dapper Casanovas who as far as their wives are concerned are socializing at their old boys' club, have only honorable intentions. What's more honorable than a quick haircut at Harrods and a couple of hours with two girls of your choice who are there to please. Hopefully it never occurred to these gents that 45 minutes before they turned up, some with flowers and some without, that the girls had been servicing someone else. And hopefully for their egos sake if it was not their first visit the girls actually remembered them, a reason to tip well or be a real kink eh!

If you miss the warning signs and are set up, "honey trapped", your world can quickly go from extreme ecstasy to extreme misery. At the low end of the scale that hot chick that promises you a night of debauchery will just take you to a shady hotel room or apartment where you'll be beaten, robbed and maybe raped by her waiting accomplices. An imaginative honey trap happened to a French businessman in 2002. He met an attractive Russian girl online and agreed to meet her in Moscow. She met him at Sheremetyevo airport and took him to a waiting car where he was kidnapped! The first his wife knew about him going to Moscow was when she received a ransom demand for $3,000,000.00. His kidnappers were not professional, and he was rescued by the Moscow police. This case made the international media, so how much damage it did to his credibility, not to mention how he would explain the situation to his wife.

At a higher level a more intricate honey trap can go on for an extended period of time until you believe it's some form of relationship, of course the sex, the more deviant the better would be videoed and then used to blackmail you for business favors or hard currency. A common criminal tactic is to pimp out a girl or boy who looks the legal consenting age for sex and then claim after the sex has taken place they are underage. That way they have a lot of leverage on the unfortunate and stupid gent who has without knowing possibly committed a serious criminal act, sex with a minor.

I do not judge others' lifestyles; I have been fortunate to experience a lot of what the world has to offer, I understand how things work and see a lot of things a lot differently than most. I tell my clients not to get into situations and environments they do not understand because things can go very wrong, very quickly. Especially in the world of the sex business, be it legal or illegal. In many cases if things go bad the police will not be interested in helping you, even if you can report the crime without being implicated in illegal activates yourself.

Always remember what I said earlier, the sex business is a business, it's all about hard currency not emotions and you are the commodity.

Counter-Surveillance Considerations

If you are serious about your personal security basic counter-surveillance procedures should be part of your daily routine. The reason you need to understand counter-surveillance is to identify anyone who has you under surveillance. In nearly all burglaries, muggings, robberies, assassinations, or kidnappings the criminals or terrorists will put their target under surveillance to assess their target's routines and the level of personal security. If you're operating in an area where professional organized criminal groups or narco terrorists are active you can be assured, they will be employing multi-layered surveillance programs the identify threats to their organizations and to identify potential targets for kidnapping or extortion.

Counter-surveillance is the base skill for all personal security and close protection programs. In this short chapter, I am going to high-light some of the main considerations for a counter-surveillance plan and detail some simple but effective street drills that will enable you to identify if you are under surveillance.

Many supposed security, tactical, close protection professionals put a lot of time, effort and money into firearms and unarmed combat training, but very few spend any time or effort on their surveillance and counter-surveillance skills.

To put things in perspective on a basic level: what weapon do you think has killed the most people? I would say a rock, since beginning of time humans have been smashing each other's heads with rocks! So, Mr. Executive Protection Specialist can be looking cool in his $500.00 suit, 3A vest and packing a .40 Glock. But if they are too busy looking cool to realize they are being watched and followed it will take little skill to come up and smash them in the back of the head with a rock, game over. Please note, unlike the movies, if you're dealing with professional criminals they will go after their target's security personnel before the actual target; remove or make an example of the security personnel and the target will be defenseless and most likely very compliant. If you can't look after yourself on a basic level, how can you expect to be able to look after others?

Professional surveillance operatives put their targets into three categories unaware, aware and professional. Most people, I would say at least 75%, fall into the unaware category, you can follow them around all day and they won't realize you're there, try it the next time you're out at the mall. About 24% of people would fall into the aware category and would realize, after a while if someone was watching or following them. The 1% left would fall into the professional category; they take active counter surveillance measures and would spot people acting suspicious, watching or following them. So, I expect most people reading this article are in the unaware category but by the time you finish reading this there is no reason not be in the professional category.

The Basics

You can start training while you're reading this chapter; look around where you are now, if you're in an office look out the window. Are there any people hanging around on the street or sitting in parked cars for no apparent reason? If they are still there in 30 minutes and there is no logical reason, what are they up to, what's their body language saying, are being they over observant? People don't hang around the streets and sit in parked cars for no reason, unless they are on surveillance or up to something!

Learning to read peoples body language is an extremely important skill, if someone is on surveillance or looking to commit a crime, chances are they will be acting differently than those around them. Most people do not pay attention to their surroundings, so if someone is over observant what are they up to?

When you are out at the mall or in a restaurant or bar, watch the people around you and try to identify what mood they are in or what type of discussion they are having with others. It should be easy to identify if a man and a woman are on a romantic date or two business people are having a heated discussion. When in a coffee shop try to determine what people are looking at on their laptops; are they concentrating or goofing around. You must learn to read body language, because this will help you identify, avoid and if necessary react to potential threats.

A basic counter-surveillance plan for your home, business or office would be simply look around the general area and identify where someone could watch you from, then keep an eye on that location from time to time. If someone is hanging around that area take note and if they are there for an extended time or regularly what are they doing?

These days if you're drawing up a counter-surveillance plan you need to take surveillance cameras into consideration. There is a vast array of affordable surveillance cameras on the market that can be used either defensively to watch potential surveillance locations you've identified or offensively by someone intent to spy on you. For example, at a very basic level, why sit outside someone's house and watch them when you can place a $100 hunting trail camera in their garden? Retrieve it after a few days and you will have photos/video of all their comings and goings. If your budget allows it, why not place a camera connected to a GSM network that will send real time images to your cell phone or email? Here I am talking about regular commercial hunting cameras available at Wal-Mart, not specialized remote surveillance cameras. But no worries, as I am sure everyone reading this regularly sweeps their gardens and parking lots for surveillance cameras, right?

I am old school and believe that you need to be able to operate with minimum equipment and support but should employ technology when you have access to it, just don't be 100% reliant on it. These days' drones are easily available to the public and can be used for surveillance and counter surveillance. Things that need to be considered when using drones is their camera quality, flight time, weather conditions they will be used in and from the good guys' point of view what the laws are on their use in your area. Even within a small scale private security operation drones could be employed for estate security for clearance, perimeter patrols and route checks etc.

To dominate the area around a location you would need to patrol it and pay special attention to potential surveillance locations, think like the criminals or terrorists and put yourself in their shoes; how would YOU watch YOURSELF? When I say patrol an area I do not mean you need to dress up in tactical gear and pretend to be RoboCop. You can patrol an area by going for a casual walk, walking a dog or taking a bicycle ride, etc. Whilst patrolling you want to be looking for people or cars that are out of place, cameras, and ground signs that people have been waiting in specific locations such as cigarette butts, trash, or trampled vegetation.

Overt patrols only draw attention and will alert your opposition that you are taking active measures, which will then up their skill level and cause them retreat to farther out positions. If you identify you are under surveillance without alerting your opposition, there are many ways to exploit the situation. How you do so will depend on the overall circumstances of the operation, your resources, and the laws which you are working under. All of this needs to be considered in your operational planning.

In urban areas surveillance operatives use as cover locations where people congregate, such as cafes, bars, bus stops or pay phones. If someone is sitting in the coffee shop across the road from your office all day they may just be working there, but if you see them on the subway or at another location, then maybe you have a stalker, private investigator, or criminal on your tail.

If you think you are under surveillance you need to establish why and who the threat is: criminals, government, a lone stalker, private investigators, or a crazy ex.

You need to do this, so you can determine their potential skill level and consider what other type of surveillance is being used against you: listening devices, remote cameras, mail being intercepted, computers being hacked or physical surveillance?

These days we must ensure our computers, smart phones and internet connections are secure; if the criminals or terrorist get access to these, for most people, they will know all personal details. I am still surprised today that a lot of people have no security on their phones or computers, post personal information, and photos on public social media accounts. I think these days it's suspicious if someone does not use social media to some extent, personally I think most platforms are safe enough, just understand whatever you post is or can become public.

Computer and network security is constantly evolving specialist industry that needs to be left to the experts, but social engineering is something everyone in the security industry needs to understand. In basic terms, social engineering is some form of confidence trick used to gather intelligence, defraud or get access to computer systems etc. A lot of successful computer hacks are down to successful social engineering operations rather than network penetrations. Social engineering operations are disguised as regular everyday happenings that fit in with the target's lifestyle. For example, the bored middle-aged CEO gets a Facebook friend request from an attractive young lady, he confirms the request and starts chatting and trying to impress her. The young ladie's Facebook profile can be a complete fraud made up by those targeting the CEO or other members of his corporation. By just confirming the friend request the CEO has given the criminals or terrorists access to a wealth of information, and will give up more in his ongoing conversations and hopefully emails from his corporate account...

Just think about how many people can access your computer, for example colleagues at your office. If you leave your computer at the office overnight can maintenance, security or cleaning staff get access to it. There have been cases of corporate espionage where private detective agencies have placed agents in the cleaning and security staff working at their targets offices, so they can access the target company's computers and trash after work hours. Most people would not consider the threat of a bumbling night shift security guard or the apparently, barely literate office cleaner downloading business data from their computer or copying confidential papers, but they should!

You cannot carry your computers around with you all the time so, one thing to do is to keep minimum information on it, keep all your sensitive information on a thumb drive or hard drive, which you can always keep on your person. Then if someone accesses your computer or if it's lost or stolen the criminals won't get any worthwhile information.

The next time you are in a coffee shop for example, without being obvious, look at what people are doing on their computers, phones and listen in to their conversations. Many people regularly work in public locations where anyone can view their computer screens, with unsecure Wi-Fi connections with the same comfort level they would have at home. When chatting with friends in public people disclose personal information all the time that could be useful to a criminal. So, remember if you can view what others are doing on their computers or phones and listen to their conversations others could do the same to you if given the opportunity.

If you believe you or your clients' computers or phones are bugged then you would need to get them cleaned, which can be costly and difficult in some locations. Another option is to use misinformation to mislead or entrap those who may be monitoring you. This could be a safer option rather than letting the criminals or terrorists know that their operation is compromised, which could force them into acting.

Street Drills

So, you must always be on the lookout for criminal surveillance and here I have listed a few simple drills, which are used by professional criminals and intelligence operatives alike. These simple drills will help you identify anyone who is watching or following you. But first let me give you an example from the mid 1990's when I was part of a commercial surveillance team in central London who's task was to watch a target that turned out to be in the professional category.

The people running the job had placed a surveillance vehicle, an old British Telecom van, across the road from the target's hotel. The target, I expect, identified the van quickly; tinted rear windows, parked in one position for an extended period etc. If I remember right on the first day the target left the hotel, jumped into a black cab and we lost him straight away due to traffic. On day two the target took the subway and went for a walk around the West End of London. He used several of the counter surveillance drills I have listed here and ripped the surveillance team apart! Those running the job resorted to placing a pseudo married couple in the hotel to try to observe what the target was doing and talking about in the bar and restaurant. Running surveillance on aware and professional targets can be extremely difficult, it's not like the movies. You should always be at the aware level but preferably professional level of awareness and it's not difficult to accomplish that!

Adapt a few of these drills to your situation, they are simple and proven.

- When walking on the street, turn around and walk back the same way you came; remember the people you walk past or anyone that stops. Also, remember to check on the opposite side of the street for anyone stopping etc. Do this several times and if you see the same person or couples more than once they may be following you.
- If you are driving do a couple of U turns, watch for anyone doing the same and the cars you pass. If you see the same car a couple of times you may be followed.
- Walk around a corner, stop, and remember the first few people that come after you. Again, do this several times and, if you see the same person more than once, they may be following you. Watch the body language of those that come around the corner after you, any flinch could be an indication you have surprised them. You can also do the same when you're driving. From a personal security point remember to always take corners wide as you never know what's waiting for you on the other side.
- Escalators are good for counter-surveillance because whilst ascending, you can have a good look around at who is behind you. A simple drill would be to go up and escalator and straight back down again, if anyone is following you they would have to do the same.
- Take special note of people waiting in parked cars, especially near your residence or office. Be especially suspicious of any unattended vans with blacked-out windows parked close to your residence or office. Vans are the most common surveillance and snatch vehicles. As the saying goes: there are only two reasons for two to be waiting in a car for no apparent reason: they are either having sex or they are on surveillance.
- Do not board trains or buses until the last minute; anyone boarding after you should be treated as suspect.
- Jump on a bus, tram or metro and jump off one stop later and see if anyone else does the same. People usually don't bother getting on a bus to go only 200 yards.
- Go into a café and covertly watch what goes on in the street. Look out for people waiting around to follow you when you leave or anyone who keeps walking past the café, they could be trying to see what you're doing. Pay special attention to locations where people are congregating for legitimate reason, such as bus stops, cafes etc...
- Walk across open spaces such as parks or squares and see if anyone is running around the outside of the open area trying to keep up with you- they must do this because there is no cover for them in the open space and the distance to go around the open space is greater than walking straight across it.
- Use reflections from windows and other surfaces to see who is behind you or use the selfie camera on your cell phone.

- Look for people who look out of place or are waiting in the same place for a long time, such as waiting at a bus stop without getting on any buses or at a payphone for an extended period.
- Be aware of people waiting in a location by themselves, especially fit, young men with short hair. Chances are they are criminals or police. Professional surveillance teams usually consist of mixed couples in their 30's to 50's. Criminals regularly use children, so be wary!
- If you think someone is following you, do not acknowledge them, just slow down and stop to look in shop windows, or go into a café and have a coffee. If you still see the person waiting around, you are most probably under surveillance.
- When you're driving, drive slowly, and take note of anyone doing the same, occasionally pull over and make note of the cars that go past you, if you see the same car more than once you might have a problem.
- If you do not want to look directly at someone who could be following you, look at their feet and remember their shoes. Very few people wear the same shoes, check this out the next time you are out. If you keep seeing the same pair of shoes at various locations, this person could be following you.
- Criminals following you may change their hair, jackets and pants etc. to try and disguise themselves but they rarely change their shoes. The same goes for jewelry or watches, it can be difficult to give a description of someone so look for distinctive jewelry, tattoos or type of cell phone or anything that makes them stand out. If the person is completely non-descript, chances are they are pros.
- If you think someone is following you check their dress to see if they could be concealing cameras or weapons. Are they always on their cell phone possibly describing your actions or taking photos? What does their body language say, do they look nervous, over observant, or as if they are concentrating to much etc.
- Be suspicious of unknown people who start conversations with you- they could be testing your reactions and personal security level.
- You need to be extra vigilant when attending any meetings. In high risk situations, these could have been set up by the opposition to photograph you or set you up to be kidnapped or assassinated. Always sweep the area for anything suspicious people or vehicles before attending the meeting.
- If you think the opposition is trying to get photos or video of you, meet in places where there is low light, like dark restaurants and stay in the shadows as most cameras will not be able to get decent pictures.
- If you believe someone is trying to get audio recordings of you, meet in a crowded place and keep your voice low. The noise from other people or traffic etc. would be picked up by any microphones and can cover your conversation.

- To check whether the person with whom you are meeting is under surveillance, turn up 5 minutes late and sweep the area for anyone suspicious. Try to take the person you're meeting with to another location and do a couple of discreet counter surveillance maneuvers along the way.
- Stop regularly to make telephone calls, or look in shop windows as this will allow you to observe your surroundings and identify anyone who may be following you.
- Use underground trains whenever available- radios and mobile phones usually don't work underground. This will cause problems for any surveillance team as they won't be able to communicate with each other.
- You must make plans on what procedures you will carry out if you are under surveillance. These will depend on where you are and the threat you are under. These days if you think you're being watched, chances are the criminals, terrorists or stalker have already tried to hack you phone or computer, so get them cleaned up and secured!

Now, from a personal security point of view if you are on the street and you seriously think you are being followed get to a safe area as soon as possible and call for someone trusted to come and pick you up. From a close protection operations point of view there are various tactics you can employ if you want to identify those following you or to warn them off, all depends on where you are and the overall operational plan.

In first world countries, you can inform the police, but I strongly expect they won't take the call seriously unless there is a domestic restraining order in place or there is a case history. If you or your client are being stalked you need to start building up evidence against the stalker, take videos and log occurrences down. If someone is watching your home or business call the police and report it, if they are not busy they may respond and question the individual etc. Which depending on the case could lead to a loitering ticket, an arrest or nothing, but a least you have a record of calling the police for your file.

I've had numerous clients over the years that have had issues with private detectives following them and watching them. If you are being stalked and harassed by private detectives call the police on them, they have no special authority, their badges just mean they are licensed if that. They cannot trespass, go through garbage, or inhibit your lifestyle etc. If the police can't help, then a written complain to their licensing authority with evidence of their actions tends to work!

This is a short chapter on what is a very important and in-depth subject and I hope it makes you think about your personal security procedures and assists you in your operational planning. Again remember: If you can't look after yourself on a basic level, how can you expect to be able to look after others!

Electronic Surveillance

Electronic surveillance is a main intelligence gathering resource for governments, criminals, terrorists and private investigators. It is easy to get hold of listening devices (bugs), bugging equipment and covert cameras from commercial outlets and many shops specialize in making and supplying this type of equipment. Today, many bugs and covert cameras can be hidden in almost any object like books, computers, mobile phones, rocks and clothing. You should always take precautions against bugs and covert cameras, especially when you are staying in hotels or moving into a new residence.

There are thousands of devices on the commercial market that claim to be able to detect bugs. However, bugs work on many different frequencies or on GSM networks and many commercially available bugs and bug detectors work on only a small sector of frequencies available. A professional criminal or terrorist will always try to use bugs that are outside of the usual frequencies or on GSM networks, so they stand less chance of detection. In addition, you must take into consideration remote controlled bugs that can be turned on and off by the listener. With most equipment you would not pick up this type of bug, because it would usually be turned off until needed, such as during a meeting. In this sector, the most expensive equipment is not always the best. If you are considering buying this type of equipment, make sure it does what the maker claims.

If your threat is from electric surveillance (ES), you should employ the services of a trusted specialist in the electronic counter-surveillance (ECM) field. Always check the credentials of the person you employ for this task and make sure he is trustworthy, also check out that his ECM kit of a professional standard. An ECM specialist should also have the equipment that is required to find bugs that are not within the usual frequency ranges. If you use the services of a commercial ECM specialist they must never be left unsupervised, there have been many cases where de-buggers have been found to be working for the opposition and planting or ignoring devices.

You should also be aware of the threat from "hard wire" devices. These do not transmit information via the airways and cannot be detected by scanners etc. A listen through a wall device is a good example of this type of device. The device could be placed on an outside of a meeting / hotel room and pick up all conversation taking place in the room andhe device could be attached directly to a recorder. There are government agencies claiming to have a micro fiber device that they can stretch for 3 kilometers and receive good quality audio and video footage.

It would be unrealistic for you to always carry around with you ECM equipment. The best defense that you have against these devices is to perform a physical search whenever you will be staying for some time in a room or moving in to a new residence. You should always carry with you such equipment as a torch and a Swiss Army type knife or tool. These basic items are all you should be adequate for a basic room search. If you anticipate that you will have to do an in-depth search always take a full search kit.

How A Bug Could Be Placed

Consider this, a criminal is targeting an executive for kidnapping. He needs to get information on the executive's moments etc. A simple tactic would be to place a listening device in the reception area of the targets office. The criminal would need to buy a simple small listening device which, could be bought over the internet or from a spy shop. The criminal would then task an associate, preferably female to enter the reception area and ask receptionists for directions etc. While talking to the receptionists the female could blow her nose and ask them to let her put her tissue in their trash can. Wrapped in the tissue would be the bug, who would ask to check a tissue someone has just blown their nose in! All going well the bug would now be in place and would pick all that the receptionists are saying. Think about it, receptionists handle a lot of sensitive information; they make appointments, book taxis and restaurants etc. A small bug could transmit for about 20 to 75 meters depending on its quality and the environment it's used in. If someone could not covertly get close enough to listen to it, a receiver attached to a digital voice activated recorder could be placed close by in a flower bed or up a drain pipe etc. GSM bugs use sim cards so can be listened in from and location globally with a phone connection.

Considerations

- Why might your client be under electronic surveillance?
- Who is the threat? Criminal, government, commercial, personal?
- What is the expected level of skill and equipment of the opposition?
- What knowledge of you does the opposition have?

Counter Procedures

- Change meeting rooms and places at short notice- this will cause problems for anyone who was planning to put you under electronic surveillance.
- Search rooms prior to meetings.

- Clear everyone from the room/area before the search and then secure the area and allow access to authorized personnel only after the search is finished.
- Upgrade the security of all areas and employ your own personnel in a counter surveillance role.
- Physically search the area for suspect vehicles which could be used as a receiving/relay point for transmissions from a bug.
- Leave enough time to search the area before the meeting starts.
- Meeting rooms should have minimal furniture as this gives the opposition less places to plant bugs.
- Search everyone entering meeting rooms for recorders or transmitters and make sure all rubbish is searched and removed.
- Check any vacant-adjoining buildings and physical search the outside of buildings.
- Perform counter-surveillance physical and electronic during meetings.
- Keep a frequency scanner on permanent scan.
- Be aware of remote controlled bugs.
- Search pictures, sockets, phones, plugs, any gifts, Place tape over screw heads, check any new furnishings, check ceiling panels, check outside the room.
- Draw curtains or close blinds before the those attending the meeting enter the room.

Cell/mobile phones can also be used as listening devices when set to auto-answer, once they are put in place the threat just calls the phone to hear what is being said in the close vicinity around the phone, what limits using cell phones is their size and battery life. The other issue with cell/mobile is that they can be hacked or have surveillance apps installed. There are many commercially available surveillance apps for cell/mobile phone monitoring. In high-crime areas where the criminals are working with the police and cell phone companies' they can monitor your calls and emails via the servers.

Another cover for planting electronic surveillance devices are burglaries, if you came home and found that your house or car had been broken into would you be more worried about what had been stolen or what had been put in place? If your car, house or hotel room has been broken into they need to be searched for electronic surveillance devices and contraband. I mentioned cars here because they are favored areas to plant listening devices as they are generally easier for the criminal or private investigator to get access to and break into than a residence. Also consider what you discuss in your car; many an extra marital affair has been discover or confirmed by a voice activated Dictaphone placed in a straying spouses car.

Dictaphone's on their own can be used by criminals as listening devices, when combined with a miniature microphone that can bought from most electrical stores they make an excellent hard wire device. Dictaphones these days can record more than seventy-two hours and the data transferred easily to a computer. Consider how easy it would be for a criminal to get access to the outside walls or roof of the location you're in now, drill a small hole through to the inside and then place the microphone in the hole. Outside the microphone wire could be camouflaged and the Dictaphone waterproofed and concealed, even buried, every few days the criminal could come by and swap the Dictaphone for one with fresh batteries and memory. The only way to find such a device would be a physical search; the $25K bug locator and the $500.00 per, hour specialist would be a waste of time and money.

Hopefully after reading this chapter you are more aware of the threat from electronic surveillance and how easy it is for even low-level criminals to use this means of gathering intelligence on an intended target.

Secrecy

Nothing is as important as secrecy. All your security plans and preparations will be worthless if the bad guys know them. Good personal and operational security begins with a clear understanding of what kind of information the criminals will be trying to learn about you, your family or business operation.

Governments must keep secret their diplomatic alliances, secret treaties and military strategies etc. Although a government may suffer a great loss because of poor security, it is hard to imagine today a situation where a nation's defenses could be completely overwhelmed by a single security leak, not so with a small-scale operation. A company might be ruined as the result of a single security leak. A family might be ambushed and kidnapped because of a single piece of information was found out by the criminals, such as home address, security procedures, routes your child takes to school or their travel itinerary.

Things that should be kept secret and restricted:
- Addresses and identity of individual employees, their families or close friends.
- Their security plans and methods of operation.
- Their transportation capabilities.
- The source's supplies.
- Available back up.
- Location of hideouts, safe houses, etc.
- Codes, signals, pass word and lines of communications.

Good personal security is a must, good team security begins with good personal security. If a person is living or traveling under their own name, they must keep information about their occupation and activities limited to those who need to know only. There is no one more completely defenseless than the individual whose personal security has been compromised.

Personal security is a 24/7 job, to some it comes almost instinctively but others can find it very hard to develop. An individual's habits and personality will have a considerable effect on their attitude towards personal security, some people will just never get it and can be a liability. Such people should not be allowed access to sensitive information or taken to high-risk locations.

The Basic Principals of Security

- **Deception:** Deception is essential to the success of all security operations, always have a cover story and be ready with feasible explanations to who you are, what you're doing and why you are doing it.
- **Avoiding attention:** One way for any individual or organization to seriously compromise their security is to attract attention. Always keep a low profile and remember that If people don't know what you are doing, they cannot counteract you.
- **Self-discipline:** Everyone must abide by the rules, if anyone disregards the security program, they could jeopardize the personal security of all involved.
- **The program:** A security program must be outlined and made clear to all personnel. Everyone must be trained and willing to work within the program.
- **Continual inspection:** The biggest thieves are usually those trusted with largest responsibilities- they have access to assets or information worth stealing. The conscientious person with the flawless record can easily deviate by their own accord or with the pressure of a little blackmail. People change and so does the importance they place on their own security, given time people will relax. This is why there is a need for everyone to be constantly inspected.
- **Fluid change:** This is best illustrated by frequent changes of meeting places, routes and operational procedures to keep the criminals guessing. This principle is necessary because, if given enough time, professional criminals can crack the security of any organization. So, old security measures must be constantly and fluidly replaced and updated.
- **Action:** If someone is not capable of obeying the security program they will need to be disciplined, they should not be trusted or only trusted with information or tasks that will not jeopardize anyone else.

You will not have a security program by following only one or more of these principles, all must be followed, and you must remain alert 24/7.

Basic Counter-Intelligence

Basic counter-intelligence increases the security of all operations and the chances of surprise in offensive operations. Your security program, even if it is for yourself, should be developed to prevent the leaking of information, or situations where criminals can extract information from you or your business. You must initially try finding criminal sympathizers already within your operation; this could be your locally recruited secretary or attorney. If you detect a sympathizer within your operation what are you going to do, fire them or feed them false information?

You should also consider why they sympathize with the criminals, is it for money or are they being threatened. Counter-intelligence can be broken down in the two practices, denial and detection.

Basic denial operations may include:
- Thoroughly brief everyone on how the criminals will try to get information on you, your personnel and your operation.
- Place a high emphasis on the security of information. People must understand to keep things on a need to know basis and not to talk about confidential subjects in public.
- Make sure all papers, old computers and communication devices etc. are properly disposed of.
- Employees should be briefed on. bars, clubs and other venues that are safe to frequent and those that are not.

Basic detection operations may include:
- Background investigations must be done on all employees, especially locals who have access to confidential information.
- Make maximum use of CCTV, covert cameras for detection and overt cameras for deterrence.
- Monitor your staff communications including e-mail and telephone calls.
- Put any staff members acting suspiciously or who seem to be living beyond their means under investigation and surveillance.

These are just some basic considerations, but they can make your security program into something that would make it extremely difficult for the bad guys to gain information on you. If they cannot get any information on you it makes their job targeting you a lot harder. Hopefully, so hard they'll go and do what we want them to do, find and easier target of which there are plenty.

Intelligence Gathering

The best way to learn how to defend something is to learn how to attack it. I wrote the below information on intelligence gathering a few years ago for a project we were dealing with in West Africa. This chapter highlights basic intelligence gathering techniques that can be used against criminals and terrorists, which can also be used against you. As you read through this think how you could be targeted and what you could do to prevent information leaks.

Intelligence Gathering

Good intelligence is the most important element in all counter insurgency (COIN) operations. Your goal is to build an accurate picture of the terrorist network, terrorist's identities, their safe houses, capabilities, sources of supplies and finances etc. Below are a few considerations on how to gain intelligence on terrorist organizations.

False Intelligence

You must always verify all information that you intercept or is supplied to you, never take things at face value. Unverified information needs to be treated as unreliable or with great caution even if the source is reliable. Sources need to be rated as to their reliability. When information is supplied think, what was the reason the source supplied it, what was their incentive to supply the information, this needs to be analyzed? Over time a sources reliability and value should become clear and they should be rewarded likewise.

Misinformation is something that can be used against you or used in your favor. The terrorists can feed you false information to lead you off their trail or into ambushes etc. That is why all information needs to be verified. If staging an operation on a sources information precautions need to be taken at all stages of the operations to avoid compromise or ambush. You can use misinformation to lure the terrorists into arrest or ambush locations, to spread confusion or discord within their organization etc. Use your imagination.

Communications

Once a terrorist suspect or supporter has been identified you can target their communications system. All terrorist organizations need to be able to communicate internally within their organization and with externally with family member and sources of supplies etc. Interception of the terrorist lines of communication is an excellent source of valuable intelligence.

1. **Mail:** Mail or written messages can be intercepted and read or modified to you needs
2. **Phones:** Land lines can be listened into and easily traced. If the terrorists are using pay phones you want to identify and patterns into which phones they are using and then bug these phones and put them under physical surveillance. Cell phones can be traced to a location within a few meters, consider them to be tracking devices.
3. **Radios:** Most commercial radio signals can be intercepted with radio scanners

Family and Friends

Most people only communicate with a small group of family, friends and associates. So, if you are looking for someone their friends and family can lead you to them, usually it is only a matter of time before someone makes contact with their family etc.

1. The mail and phones of the family and associate of the terrorist can be monitored.
2. The family and associate can be placed under physical surveillance.
3. The business and home addresses of the family and associate of the terrorist can be put under physical surveillance, mail and phone lines monitored and listening devices placed within the buildings. If terrorists are spotted they can be followed or arrested etc. Also monitor the electricity or water bills etc. for the building, if the electricity or water usage goes up or there is an increase in food deliveries etc. possibly someone could be hiding in the building.
4. Cars of the family and associate of the terrorist can be fitted with tracking and listening devices.

Locals and Neighbors

Locals and Neighbors of the terrorist, their family and associates can prove to be good sources of intelligence. Send a socially skilled operative to speak with them paying special attention to anyone who shows a dislike for the terrorist, their family and associates.

Media

You should monitor all media sources such as newspapers and the internet. Any reporters who are writing stories about the terrorist organization should be monitored.

Documents

Any sized or stolen document need to be analyzed. Even the smallest pieces of information should not be over looked.

Supplies

All terrorist organizations need to be supplied with weapons, ammunition, food, medical equipment, gasoline and cash etc. You want to identify the terrorist's sources of supplies. These sources can then be monitored, and the supplies tracked or modified.

Routes or Areas Frequented

Suspected routes used by the terrorists and locations they frequent for social activity etc. should be monitored or ambushed. If terrorists are spotted they can be followed or arrested etc.

Rewards

Rewards can be offered for information on the terrorists. All information would need to be verified and rewards would need to be paid if the information supplied is credible. Not paying rewards would lead to the program soon losing credibility.

Spying Operations

Where possible a network of informers (sources) should be established, you should seek to recruit people who could have information on the terrorists or are close to them. Methods of recruitment for sources varies greatly from person to person and depends a lot on their personality and reason for giving up information on the terrorists. Our initial phase is to find people who have a grudge against the terrorists; they could be owed money, be ex-lovers etc. They could possibly still be in contact with the terrorists or be able to establish communications and could be seeking revenge or compensation.

The second group of potential recruits would be those who under normal circumstances would not be considered to be sources of information on the terrorist organization. These are people who would need to be persuaded to provide information on the terrorists. If you believe someone could provide you with information and be a semi-reliable source you would need to compile a life style check on the person and identify anything that could be used against them. Such as, debits, vices (sex, drug or alcohol use, gambling etc.), extra marital affairs, criminal activity etc. that they would not want others to know about and would be willing to provide information on the terrorist to prevent others finding out about. A little pressure can sometimes work wonders!

Everyone in your network should be offered payment of some kind. If you identify a potential source has debts, then money could be the only incentive they need to provide information on the terrorists. Any exchanges of cash or assets with sources needs to be videoed, this vides could use in the future if the source becomes uncooperative.

Source Security

The identifications of your sources must be kept on a need to know basis, code names need to be allocated and used as soon as a potential source is identified. The personal security of the source and their family needs to be considered always. If a source is compromised, they need to be informed and relocated ASAP. If a source is killed or kidnapped it can lead to fear in other sources who may become uncooperative. If people know they are safe and will be looked after they will be more productive. All files and evidence on sources needs to be kept secure, encrypted and disposable.

The Placing Undercover Operatives

This where one of your operatives tries to infiltrate the terrorist organization. Your operative would need to appear to be a sympathizer to the terrorist cause and have a similar interest to those he is seeking to become friends with. When a suitable terrorist or supporter is identified the operative would try to strike up a relationship with them. The initial approach would not be about the terrorists cause but should be about a common interest such as soccer etc. You would need to compile a life style check on the terrorist and identify any thing that could assist the operative in hooking them. A suitable time and location for this first approach would need to be determined, this is when things can get off to a good start or no start at all. Over time it would be the operatives job to win the confidence of the terrorist or supporter, depending on how the relationship developed depends on how the terrorist could be used. If they are loyal to their cause should hopefully be able to supply valuable information, if they are disgruntled with their cause they could be turned or guided to cause friction with in the terrorist organization. How involved the operative will get with the terrorists will depend on the situation and their safety, if an operative is left in place dealing with the terrorists for an extended period there is a chance they themselves could turn to the terrorist cause, the mental wellbeing of the operative needs to be closely monitored.

Threat Assessments (TA)

The Threat Assessment (TA) is the most important of all the procedures carried out in any security or business operation but even the most basic TAs are regularly overlooked. The reason for a TA is to identify anything that might threaten you, your team and your overall operation. People carry out basic forms of TAs all the time: Which bars are safe to drink in, where is it safe to walk at night, do I need locks on the windows of my home etc.

A threat assessment must identify all threats that you are exposed to whether it is physical assault, injury, terrorism, black mail, being embarrassed or discredited, health problems, loss of assets or dangerous weather conditions etc. When you identify a threat, you must take procedures to minimalism it. In the world of security operations, most people only look for the threat of physical assault, but you must look as deeply as you can and cover every angle.

Consider this, a security company is looking after a client who is being threatened by a potentially violent ex-business partner. The client is married with children. The children have several pets: a cat and a dog. The client lives in a two-story house surrounded by a garden. The security company has identified the threat and decided to install CCTV and provide the client with a team of armed bodyguards. The ex-business partner decides to strike at the client. One night he throws bits of meat he has poisoned over the wall into the client's garden, which the client's pets eat. When the client and his family wake up in the morning, the pets are dead, and his children are very upset. 1-0 to the opposition. Could this have been avoided, maybe, maybe not. I doubt that many people would consider that a client's family pets would need to be considered in a TA. As I am sure you will agree, such an attack as I have described would be a psychological assault on the client and by upsetting his family would most probably have more of an effect than just physically assaulting him.

When first compiling a TA, you need to get as much information as possible, past, present and future on the person or organization on whom you will be compiling the assessment. Most people may not want to include certain things like extra marital affairs, drug or drinking habits or similar activities. However, it is vitally important that these are included, as they are a source of many potential problems. It would make sense in a lot of business operations to compile and profile staff and family members.

When you compile the threat assessment and a threat is identified, you must find out as much about it as is possible- whether it is an illness or organized criminals. You will need to locate sources of information for your research including media cuttings, libraries, trade catalogues, directories, public records and the Internet. You need to assess what action has been taken against you from a threat: verbal abuse, physical assault, stealing trash, tapping your phones or previous heart attacks.

On the follow pages is an example of a personal / threat profile that can be used to build up information on the person you are compiling the TA on, this could be yourself, client or a criminal. If the information compiled is used properly it can help you to predict the criminal's plan of action and it will also aid law enforcement agencies in apprehending them. Not everything in the following checklist will apply to everyone and this is only a guide.

I have also included two threat assessments I compiled for clients; the first was a crime prevention assessment on a residence and the other was for a yacht going to the Eastern Aegean and Western Turkey. From these you should be able see things that need to be taken into consideration when compiling threat assessments. Remember, all TA and profiles need to be kept strictly confidential.

Example: Personal Threat Profile

Date   /   /   File Number:
1. Surname:
2. First names:
3. Alias:
4. Title: Mr/Ms/Mrs:
5. Date of birth:
7. Height:
8. Weight:
9. Build:
10. Complexion:
11. Eye color:
12. Hair color:
13. Handicaps:
14. Scars and tattoos:
15. Fingerprints taken:
16. Ethnic background:
17. Nationality and passport number:
18. Photographs:
19. Preferred jewelry & clothing:
20. Occupation:
21. Earnings:

22. Marital status:
23. Home address:
24. Type of residence
25. Who else lives there:
26. Home phone number:
27. Home e-mail:
28. Mobile phone number:
29. Description of vehicles used:
30. Business addresses:
31. Business phone numbers:
32. Business fax numbers:
33. Business e-mail:
34. Other addresses:
35. Other phone numbers:
36. Other fax numbers:
37. Active on what social networking sites
38. State of health:
39. Medication needed:
40. Recreational user of illegal or prescription drugs
41. Doctors name and contact details:
42. Duress and stress signals:
43. Places frequented by threat, both professionally and privately:
44. Languages spoken:
45. Lawyer's name and contact details:
46. Financial status:
47. Any bad debts, if yes to whom:
48. Banks used:
49. Religion:
50. Religiously active:
51. Criminal record:
52. Known current criminal activities and affiliations:
53. Known to law enforcement agencies:
54. Mode of operation:
55. Known personal and business associates:
56. Known opponents/enemies:
57. Future goals:
58. Sexual orientation both public and private:
60. Political & freemason affiliations:
61. Eccentricities & habitual behavior:
62. Details of spouse or partner:
63. Details of children and other family members:
64. Details of other direct family, including aliases and maiden names:
65. Extra marital affairs, full details of whom with:

Example: Building Assessment

Date: ## /## /####   File Number: #########

The front of the building, East Side
The front entrance to the building is completely open with no visible security or deterrents to trespassers. Anyone can walk off the street and up to the apartments.

Possible procedures that could be put in place to deter trespassers include:
- Properly placed lights that illuminate all dark areas. On the evening I viewed the building, there were lights out in one of the stairway; this could also be a safety concern for tenants/guests and a liability concern for the building management.
- Security cameras could be placed to cover the main entrance or dummy security cameras could be placed in obvious locations to act as deterrent to possible trespassers.
- Signs could be placed in obvious locations stating that the building has security cameras, trespassers will be prosecuted, etc.

Rear and side perimeters
There did not seem to be any fences or barriers around the building that could stop a possible trespasser. The walls and fences would be easy to climb or cross for the average person.

Possible procedures that could be put in place to deter trespassers include:
- Properly placed lights, possibly on motion detectors can be placed in all dark areas.
- As with the front of the building, cameras and signs can be used to deter possible trespassers.
- The perimeter fencing needs to be replaced with something that will stop trespassers. There is no point having locked gates, if people can just jump a wall or fence a few yards away.

Walkways: There is nothing stopping people walking from the street onto the 1st floor walkways. Lockable gates could possibly be placed at the bottom of the steps leading to the walkways.

Apartments
- The doors of the apartments need to be fitted with good locks and inspected to ensure that the locks cannot be opened through a close by window. The door frames also need to be inspected to ensure they are solid. All locks on external doors need to be changed after tenants leases are expired and

before new tenants take over the apartment; I believe this is a required under Florida law.
- The apartment windows are in no way secure and are easily opened from the outside. These windows need to be replaced.
- The shutters on the inside of the windows could be alarmed and would provide warning for occupants of an intruder gaining access to the apartment. The shutters themselves are flimsy and could not stop anyone trying to gain access to the apartment but some form of dead bolt could be put in place to deter anyone from using excessive force to gain entry.
- Internal alarms could be used but it must be remembered these only alert others during a break in, they do not prevent break-ins. If alarms are to be put in place, they must be services and tested regularly.

Conclusion

In my professional opinion, the building and the apartments security level is extremely low. I personally would not be comfortable leaving valuable assets or having close friends, etc., living in the building. The main weakness is the easy accessibility to the apartments from the street and the ease that access to the apartments can be gained through the windows.

These days with crime rates on the increase the building management and landlords need to understand that they are legally liable for the security and safety of their tenants.

Example: Threat Assessment for a mega-yacht traveling to the Eastern Aegean and Western Turkey

Date: ## /## /2008   File Number: #########

Overview

The Eastern Aegean and Western Turkey areas are considered as the meeting points of Europe and Asia. This area has been important to trade since biblical times. The Eastern Aegean leads to the Sea of Marmora, that connects to the Black Sea, the route through the Bosphorus strait and the Dardanelles is now a vital artery for oil coming from Central Asia.

The Eastern Aegean is a politically complicated area due to the disputes between Greece and Turkey over various islands and tracks of sea. The Aegean Sea has about 1,415 islands and islets, of which 1,395 belong to Greece.

Maritime Crime

Although acts of maritime piracy in the Eastern Aegean seem to be extremely rare in modern times, petty crime should be expected to be at the regular level. That said, in January 1996 a passenger ferry was hijacked in the Black Sea by Chechen terrorist for 4 days. Due to the ongoing anti-terrorist operations in the Caucasus, Iraq and Afghanistan, there is a potential threat of high profile hijackings to publicize the terrorists causes.

Shore Side Crime

Street crime figures are relatively low in Turkey, although it is on the increase in large urban areas. As in other large metropolitan areas throughout the world, common street crimes include pick pocketing, purse snatching, and mugging. Be wary of approaches from strangers offering to change money or offering tea, juice, alcohol, or food, which may be drugged. Two common drugs used are Nembutal and Benzodiazepine which, when used incorrectly, can cause death. In 2007 a high number sexual assaults on foreigners, including rape, were reported in coastal tourist areas in South Western Turkey.

While walking or shopping beware of pickpockets who operate in any crowded place such as on a bus, tram, metro or entrances to busy locations where people are packed close together, guard your bag, wallet, camera, jewelry, wrist watch, and anything else of value. Other street crime methods include bag-slashes who get behind or beside you in a crowded place, slash your bag or pocket with a razor blade and collect your valuables. If they are good and they usually are, you won't see or feel a thing. Bag-snatchers are often young boys, they will grab your bag and run, if your bag is snatched do not to pursue the thief, even young boys in Turkey often carry knives and can be dangerous.

There are many cases of tourists being invited to visit clubs or bars, only to be vastly overcharge on drinks. For example, a couple may go into one of these places and order a drink. When they are presented with the bill, however, they find it to be for a thousand dollars. When they protests they are confronted by a couple of thugs who shows them the price list for drinks, which is well-hidden behind the bar. It is not unusual for a glass of Coke to be 3 to 4 hundred dollars. How things develop will depend on the club and the victims. In most cases the victim will have their wallets emptied and may be escorted to an ATM machine and instructed to draw out more money or just beaten and robbed. If there is more than one victim, one may be held in the venue while the other is sent to get more money.

Public transport Caution should be used when using public transport. Trams are a favorite location for pick-pockets and bag slashes. Overcharging by taxi drivers, particularly by those in popular tourist areas is common. Pay attention to what denomination of bill you are using to pay for the fare, taxi drivers switching money and claiming you gave a smaller denomination than what you thought is a common scam. Only utilize taxis with meters, sit in the back seat and do not accept food or drink from the driver. Try to ensure the drive sticks to the main roads, if you are uncomfortable with the driver pay them and get out the car when safe to do so.

Driving When renting motor vehicles outside of EU and US stick to the main international companies such as Hertz etc. The safety standard of rental vehicles may not be the same as EU and US and driving may be more hazardous. In many developing countries, if you are involved in a traffic accident involving locals you will be at fault just because you are a foreigner.

Counterfeits
Counterfeit and pirated goods are widely available in Turkey, many of which are produced within the country. Counterfeits can include designer clothes, sunglasses, DVDs, software, scents, toothpaste, etc. Buying such products may be illegal under local law, which may not be rigorously enforced until the local authorities just want to make a statement. Bringing counterfeit and pirated goods to the EU and US may result in forfeitures and fines. Using counterfeit deodorants, toothpastes etc. also have health risks.

There have been two cases in Altinkum within the past few months of counterfeit British 20-pound notes being reported by money changers. In both cases those accused, British citizens, were arrested and imprisoned until their court hearings. It seems strange that these two cases would occur in the same area of Turkey within a short period of time with the accused in both cases being apparently unrelated. Always use established banks to change money, because many small bureau-de-changes are used by organized crime as fronts for money laundering operations.

Police and the Law
The police and judicial system has a reputation for being hard and human rights violations are common. In tourist areas the police will be more accommodating to tourists but not forgiving where crime is concerned. Convictions of foreigners sets good examples that the police are doing their job and for tourists to behave. In some areas crimes such as physical and sexual assaults on tourists by locals may not be taken seriously by the local police or the blame laid on the tourist's actions. This is where making contact with your local embassies and consulates is important to report such crimes and indifference of the judicial system

Basic regulations and laws (UK Foreign Office)
- There is now a smoking ban on all forms of public transport (trains, ferries and taxis) and in outdoor venues (including stadiums and playgrounds). Transitional arrangements are in place for cafes, bars and restaurants; they too will come under the smoking ban in July 2009. You risk being fined 62 YTL if you are caught smoking in a designated smoke-free area.

- Turkey has strict laws against the use, possession or trafficking of illegal drugs. If you are convicted of any of these offences, you can expect to receive a heavy fine or a prison sentence of 4 to 24 years.
- The export of antiquities is prohibited and carries a prison sentence from five to ten years. The use of metal detectors is against the law.
- Dress modestly if visiting a mosque or a religious shrine.
- It is illegal not to carry some form of photographic ID in Turkey. It is therefore advisable to carry a photo copy of your passport with you at all times.
- Do not take photographs near military or official installations. You should seek permission before photographing individuals.
- Homosexuality is not illegal but is not widely tolerated: public displays of affection could result in prosecution for public order offences.
- It is an offence to insult the Turkish nation or the national flag, or to deface or tear up currency.

The Turkish Mafia

Organized crime has long established roots in Turkey and the Turkish Mafia has a brutal reputation and is one of the main players in the heroin business. Turkey is and always been an established trade route between Asia, Middle East and Europe. It is now an establish trafficking crossroads for Heroin heading in to EU and synthetic drugs heading into Asia. In recent years Turkey has also become a major route for people traffickers moving people into Western Europe from Asia. Once in Turkey the goods to be trafficked, be they people, cigarettes, drugs or counterfeit bathroom products start or continue their journey west via land or more likely by sea from Turkey's Sothern or Western coastline.

Turkey is also a major market in the domestic and international sex trafficking trade. Usually women from the former soviet states are brought to Turkey knowingly to work in the sex trade or on false pretenses and enslaved. From Turkey the women are trafficked internationally.

Prostitution is legal under Turkey's legal system. Prostitutes have mandatory weekly health checks and are issued identity cards by the local authorities. They operate out of brothels that are guarded by the local police. Note: There is a large transsexual and transvestite community in Turkey the vast majority of whom work in the sex industry.

Terrorism

Russian peace keeping operations in the Republic of Georgia and the Caucasus
There is little chance of terrorist incidents related to the military actions in the Republic of Georgia. There has been over the years numerous terrorist incidents in Turkey in protest or Russian anti-terrorist operations in Chechnya and Dagestan

against Muslim extremists. Both Russia and Georgia are orthodox Christian countries, so the Islamic community has little interest. The separatists in South Ossetia and Abkhazia are controlled by Russia as the Georgian's are controlled by the US, any acts of terrorism would be counterproductive for both sides causes and would not be tolerated by Russia or US.

- Turkey, the PKK and Iraq the issues with Turkey and the Kurd's of Eastern Turkey date back to after the first world war, in the 1970's the PKK (Kurdish Workers Party) was formed. The PKK are an active terrorist organization and close links with the Kurdish Peshmerga militia that are the de facto army of northern Iraq. This has led to Turkish forces regularly mounting ground and aerial operations into Northern Iraq to target active terrorist groups who have sanctuary there. The war between turkey and the Kurdish terrorists has been a low intensity dirty war that has estimated to have cost 40,000 lives. This conflict is likely to continue well into the future.
- Terrorist kidnappings During the early and mid-1990s, the PKK kidnapped foreign tourists in southeast Turkey, including 19 seized in eight separate incidents on July 5, 1993. In each case, the foreign tourists were well-treated and eventually released unharmed. Since then, kidnappings have been rare until recently when three German climbers were taken hostage in Eastern Turkey. They were released unharmed after Turkish military units pursed the terrorists into Iraq. As Turkey pressures the PKK in Northern Iraq and the US and NATO forces continue the war on terror kidnapping for publicity by Muslim groups is an active threat to those visiting Turkey.
- Hijacking of airplanes Hijacking is more common in Turkey than in most other countries. Turkey is home to various terrorist and criminal organizations from Islamic groups, left wing radicals to the Albanian Mafia. One recent case in August 2007 a flight that was Hijacked in northern Cyprus was diverted to Antalya in southern Turkey where all passages were released unharmed, as is the case with the majority of hijackings in Turkey.
- Bombings and Attacks Over the past few years terrorist bombing and attacks have become a regular occurrence in Turkey. Targets have included buses, banks, restaurants, hotels and foreign embassies in areas such as Istanbul, Izmir, Mersin, Cesme, Antalya, Kusadasi, Marmaris and Ankara. Many of the devices that have been used have been small and the attacks motive is to dissuade foreign investment, tourism and publicize the terrorists causes. When visiting tourist areas always be vigilant and have your procedures prepared for how to react to a terrorist incident.

Terrorist and bombing incidents include:
- 21 August 2008, a car bomb exploded in a residential area of Izmir, injuring 11 military and police personnel.

- 7 August 2008, 3 people were injured in a mortar attack on a military barracks in Uskudar, Istanbul.
- 27 July 2008, 17 people were killed and many wounded in two explosions in the Gungoren shopping district of Istanbul.
- 9 July 2008, Three police officers and three gunmen were killed in an attack on the US consulate in Istanbul.
- 3 January 2008, Six people are killed and more than 60 wounded in a car bomb attack on a military bus in the south-eastern city of Diyarbakir.
- 2 October 2007, two explosions in Izmir killed one person and injured five others and a further explosive device did not detonate.
- 11 September 2007, Police defused a large vehicle bomb in the Kurtulus district in Ankara.
- 11 July 2007, an explosion occurred outside the District Governor's office in the Bahçelievler district of Istanbul injuring two.
- 10 June 2007, an explosion occurred in a shopping district in the Bakirkoy district of Istanbul injuring 14 people.
- 22 May 2007, Six people are killed and more than 90 injured in a suicide bombing at the entrance to a shopping centre in Ankara.
- 5 November 2006, Three soldiers are killed and 14 others wounded when a roadside mine explode beside a military convoy in south-eastern Turkey.
- 2 October 2006, Fifteen people are injured in a blast at a cafe in Izmir, Turkey's third largest city.
- 12 September 2006, Eleven people are killed, eight of them children, in a bomb blast in a park in Diyarbakir, a city in the country's south-east.
- 28 August 2006, Three people are killed and at least 20 hurt in an explosion in the resort of Antalya. Later, 21 others are injured in three explosions in the southern resort of Marmaris. Another six people are injured in an explosion near the local government's office in the Istanbul district of Bagcilar.
- 4 August 2006, Thirteen people are injured in two bomb attacks in southern Turkey. The first bomb explodes near a bank in the city of Adana. The second blast occurs minutes later at a nearby construction site.
- 25 June 2006, Four people are killed and 25 injured in an explosion near a restaurant in the resort of Antalya. Initial investigations suggest a gas canister exploded, but it is not known if this was an accident.
- 15 June 2006, An explosion near a bus station in central Istanbul injures three people. Officials say an explosive device was hidden in a rubbish bin in the busy Eminonu district.
- 3 June 2006, Fourteen people are injured in an explosion outside a shopping centre in the port city of Mersin. The blast is said to have been caused by a remote-controlled bomb.

- 16 April 2006, Thirty-one people are hurt in an explosion in the Bakirkoy district of Istanbul. The blast appears to have been caused by a bomb left in a trash can near a shop.
- 5 April 2006, Two people are injured in an explosion at the local offices of the ruling Justice and Development Party (AKP) in Istanbul.
- 31 March 2006, One person dies and 13 others are injured when a bomb explodes inside a rubbish bin near a bus stop in the Kocamustafapasa district of Istanbul.
- 15 March 2006, Two people are injured in an explosion outside an HSBC bank in southern city of Diyarbakir.
- 13 February 2006, Eleven people are hurt in an explosion in front of a supermarket in the Bahcelievler suburb of Istanbul. A Kurdish terrorist group claims responsibility.

Conclusions
- Proper plans need to put into place to deal with all emergencies while at sea and shore side.
- Personal security needs to be taken seriously by all personnel.
- Personnel should have good communication with them at all times and know the contact numbers, separate from their cell phones, for the MY and other crew members.
- Shore side crew should regularly check in with the MY.
- Emergency rendezvous points and routes need to be arranged as well as emergency methods of transport to the Emergency rendezvous points.
- Medical emergencies need to be planned for. Remember, medical facilities may not be up to the standard encountered in the US or EU.

Emergency service numbers for Turkey
- Fire: 110
- Medical Emergency: 112 or 144
- Police: 155
- Gendarme: 156
- Coast Security: 158

Emergency service numbers for Greece
- Fire: 199 or 112
- Medical Emergency: 166 or 122
- Police: 100 or 112
- Coast Security: 108

List of relevant Embassies and Consulates in Greece and Turkey attached

Example: Threat assessment on ######### in #########, Dominican Republic

11 October 2006

This assessment has been compiled by two Risks Inc. operatives, who were at the location from 1600 hrs, 6 October 2006 to 0900, 9 October 2006.

This assessment will cover potential threats to the physical security of ######### staff/clients and also additional threats to the overall ######### project as seen at this time. If the project progresses, threat assessments will need to be regularly compiled.

Orlando Wilson
Risks Inc.

Overall Considerations

Due Diligence

We were led to believe no due diligence had been compiled on anyone involved in the project. This needs to be done on all investors, buyers and local assets.

Intellectual Property Security

We did not see or hear anything to suggest that there has been any consideration for the protection of the project's intellectual property. We expect information about the project that has been passed to local assets is now common knowledge to those with potential interests in the project.

Communications

It is common knowledge in DR (Dominican Republic) that all phone, fax, e-communications are monitored, and this information can be bought by those with the right contacts. If the project's local consoles have not informed you of this from the start of the project, we would doubt their loyalty.

For serious international communication, e-mail encryption is a must and the project's computer server must be housed in a secure location. There are various methods and equipment available to assist with secure phone and fax communications.

For communications between the project's staff, we suggest the use of radios; there were areas where cell phone coverage was not good. In time, base stations should be located at the ######## site and the chosen accommodation location. These would need to be monitored while personnel are on the ground

First Aid & Medical Considerations

We did not see that any consideration had been given to what to do in the case of a medical emergency. Medical facilities in DR can be basic; an in-depth assessment needs to be done on what medical facilities are in the area of the ######## site and accommodation location.

The ######### site should have first aid trained personnel and a comprehensive first aid kit on location whenever there are visitors/staff present. The state of the ######## site at this time could make a casualty evacuation difficult. Visitors and staff travelling the ######## site should always have a first aid kit in their vehicles.

There are cases of foreigners contracting malaria and dengue fever from mosquitoes. The relevant precautions need to be taken to prevent infection.

Medical insurance will need to be arranged for staff and details of locally accepted policies compiled for visitors.

A full medical assessment needs to be completed, if you are dealing with VIPs; the individuals and their insurance companies will expect you to have done this.

General Physical Security

Airport Pick Ups

All pickups from the airport should be kept low profile for staff and clients. The project needs to acquire its own vehicles and trusted drivers for this service. It would make sense not to use the ######## name on signs when collecting staff and clients; basic lettered signs should be used and changed on a regular basis. This prevents signs being copied and your staff and clients being taken away and robbed or kidnapped, et c.

We would suggest you speak to airport personnel and have the project drivers meet staff and clients directly at the exit from the airport to save them being harassed by taxi drivers, et c. For VIP clients, a more discreet procedure for entering and exiting the airport will need to be devised. We expect the airport staff would be happy to assist with implementing this for a fee.

Primary and secondary routes need to be select form the airport to the accommodation. We saw the routes are limited but need to be varied as much as possible. For client pickups, we could suggest a Spanish speaking assistant to be with the driver to help with any problems that may occur on the route. The vehicle should have good communications to keep those at the accommodation location informed of pick up, leaving the airport, any problems etc. A second vehicle needs to be at hand to recover the clients in the case of a break down or accident.

For VIP clients, a security person or team should be available in a separate vehicle.

Accommodation Security
The hotel ####### appeared to be a well-run hotel in a security-gated complex that should keep out most petty-criminals. One area that had limited security was the beach area; walking into the hotel from there would be easy. The hotel staff were polite and well-mannered but we saw no security personnel and no firearms.

If the hotel is to be regularly used, staff and clients need to be located in close proximity on the second or third floor and armed plain clothed security personnel should be in manning the hallway 24/7. This would be minimal cover and would be expected by VIP clients.

In the future, if the project gets going, and sorts out its own accommodation, full security procedures will need to be implemented. Security should be a major consideration in site selection.

Places of Entertainment
Reputable and hygienic places of entertainment for staff and clients need to be taken into consideration. An assessment of restaurants and clubs needs to be compiled; not only security needs to be taken into account but also the hygiene of the venue.

While at dinner with the project's local attorney, a large rat was seen walking around the roof of the restaurant. Such a thing could prove to be extremely embarrassing if entertaining clients and can also lead to illness etc.

Recreational transportation for staff and clients' needs to be arranged. A list of reputable tax/car companies should be compiled. For VIP clients, suitable cars, drivers and security should be available.

Route from Hotel ####### to ####### Site
It is our understanding that there is one road to the ######## site from the accommodation location, which takes about an hour to drive. This road will need to be driven and a threat assessment compiled.

Helicopters are the best option for moving staff and clients between locations but arrangements need to be made in case of bad weather or if mechanical problems occur with the helicopter. Due to the state of DR roads a 4X4 vehicle is suggested.

The ######## Site

The ######## site has no effective security; we expect the two guards we saw are only present or awake when there are visitors. They were not alert or well-presented and in no way install confidence in their ability.

The ######## site has no perimeter fence that can keep out intruders and we expect the site perimeter has never been patrolled or checked. From the small section we drove past on the road to #######, we saw several areas that look as if they were being used to gain access to the site. The site needs a perimeter fence that can keep out trespassers. All entry points need to be blocked off or manned by competent personnel.

Just driving the main site roads we saw tracks that seem to be used, as well as evidence of horse hoof prints. People have free access to this site. Due to the heavy bush and foliage it would be easy for people to be on the site without being spotted. At the location of the show houses, there were signs that people had been in them recently.

There is also free access to the site from the sea and harbor area. The entrance to the projects part of the harbor area needs to be buoyed off and a small boat made available for security patrols. This boat could also be used for showing clients the waterways.

Due to the complete lack of any perimeter security and dense foliage on the site, it is easy for petty criminals to commit express robberies on the project's staff working at the site or clients viewing the site. More serious crimes would be just as easy to commit.

We would strongly suggest that all staff and client visits to the site are proceeded by advance security and until there is decent perimeter security all senior management, clients and VIPs, at least, are accompanied by professional armed security personnel while viewing the site.

Reliable vehicles need to be in place at the site for viewing clients and security patrols. ATVs could make a better option for security patrols.

The Security Team

It is quite obvious at this point in time security has in no way been considered in this project. Due to the situation in DR and the high profile of this project all senior staff members and clients should be accompanied by armed security when not in secure areas.

We would suggest the security team to be a combination of ex-pats and local personnel. The minimum number of operational ex-pats we would recommend would be 2 for the first stages of the project and in time expanding this to a team of 4. The ex-pats would be responsible for executive protection, co-ordination of locals and special tasks.

A well-connected and controllable Dominican security company needs to be employed for the provision of executive protection personnel and regular security personnel. The Dominican personnel would need to be well trained and equipped. The management of the company would need to be well-connected in Santo Domingo to ensure things ran smoothly with local police and military agencies. At this point we would estimate approximately 8 to 12 local security and executive protection personnel are required.

The operational procedures and orders for the security team would need a lot of in-depth planning. Issues that would need to be considered would include the provision of firearms permits, et c., for ex-pats.

Other Threats
The main threats we see to the ######## projects are what is going on behind the scenes at local and national level. This is a high profile project and to our knowledge has had problems in the past. DR has a reputation for corruption at all levels, especially where large projects are concerned. We speak from experience!

Money Laundering
We were surprised to hear that apparently no precautions have been considered to prevent ######## property being bought for money laundering purposes. This could be a major threat to the whole project. One sale paid for with money from an illicit source could lead to property seizures and problems with law enforcement agencies in DR and U.S. We expect the DR side of things could be put right but it would be costly. If you have competition in this project, this is one angle that could be used against you.

Local Assets
We met with the project's local attorney, "Jesus," and from the start our impressions were not favorable. He stated he had never dealt with a contract of this size before and did not have an office in Santo Domingo; he had had a practice in Santo Domingo but it failed. To be taken seriously in DR, he would need a Santo Domingo office as this where the politics goes on and where deals are done. With a

project with the potential size of ########, you will need seriously connected local attorneys and consuls to prevent problems and ensure things run smoothly.

It appears that "Jesus" has been acting as the project manager un-supervised. We strongly doubt that in the period this project has been dormant that he has been doing nothing but waiting for you to get funding, without looking for other ways to line his pockets.

When asked about the security for the ######## site, he stated there were good security personnel in place and that no one had access to the site. We know for a fact he was talking complete and utter rubbish. When asked about security guards for the site, he stated they were looking to use a Bulgarian-run local security company. At one point, he also stated that 2 years ago, one company had bought land near the ######## site on which to set up a factory to produce furniture for the project. When asked why this company thought it was going to get the contract, he was not able to answer the question. We expect he sold them the land and guaranteed them the contract. Problems can occur if contracts have been guaranteed to vendors and they are not granted.

When the subject of the peninsular across from the ######## site was raised "Jesus" stated he had heard that there had recently been Russians asking about the sale of the land, he stated he did not know who they were. Later in the meeting he stated the Russians had bought property in DR 3 years ago.

"Jesus" stated that he is hiring new attorneys for the ######## project, all of whom- from what we heard- are young and female, pretty but with little legal experience. It was also interesting to hear one was a native Russian. He also stated one of his attorneys and himself had recently been approached by "####". As things progress you can expect these approaches to happen a lot more frequently and you must monitor local staff.

One potential problem that needs to be assessed is the town of ########. If the project takes off, the property prices in the area will increase greatly and, from what we saw, the majority of this town are not the wealthiest. We would expect this to lead to property owners evicting local renters, et c. This could lead to political, media and civil problems, if not taken into consideration beforehand.

We would strongly suggest interviewing all local assets that have been connected with the project to determine if they have been working in your interests and not leaking information or contract details, et c. "Jesus" needs to be aggressively interviewed about his official and unofficial dealings concerned with this project.

Due diligence needs to be completed on all local assets. Special attention needs to be paid to the financial dealings of local attorneys to ensure none of their previous business dealings or property deals have been illicit or have involved laundered money.

Everyone involved in any previous problems where money for concessions have been given or granted needs to be investigated. Special attention would need to be paid to these people's personal financial transactions.

Conclusions
The potential threats to the ######## project that we see are varied and numerous. The overall threat level of this project is high.
The general threat to the physical security of staff and clients is medium and should be at the normal level for those visiting DR. The threat to senior management will greatly increase as the project develops and political or corruption related problems occur

The threat from corruption is extremely high at all levels. This should be constantly monitored and expected. Without strong Dominican attorneys and consuls, the threat from corruption is greatly increased.

Estimated budget
A rough estimate for a security budget for the first 12 months of this project is $##0,000, 00.

Orlando Wilson
11 October 2006

The Problems of International Training Projects

I am sat at JFK Airport in New York writing this and I am waiting to catch a flight to the Middle East where I will teach a seminar for members of a National police force. I will stay in a nice hotel, be driven around and be decently paid, this is a far cry from 25 years ago when I was a 17 year old recruit turning up for basic British Army Infantry training at Depot Litchfield. Over the years I have provided security and training services to a wide variety of private and government client in Western and Eastern Europe, US, Latin America and Africa. And every job and location tend's to have their own individual problems!

The first thing I take into consideration when approached for a contract is who the clients are and if they are times wasters, which over 90% are. Also, what it is they want exactly, and can they afford it I regularly get emails from people wanting a vast array of course with money not being a problem, these tend to be the dreamers and the wannabes. When I believe someone is a serious client then we need to confirm they are who they say they are.

Several years ago, I was approached by a police training institute from Mexico, where my company and I have worked numerous times. We were at the stage of waiting for the plane tickets to arrive, luckily for us they did not. A week or so later we saw the media reports that the institute had been raided and its official's and others in the state associated with the local police had been arrested by federal police due to connections to the Drug Cartels. These days you have to be very careful, especially when operating in countries where government corruption is high!

When I write proposals, I expect that the training programs will change if we get the contract due to facilities, equipment and team or local politics. But if the flight tickets and retainer arrives we deal with the expected issues when we get to the location and the training starts.

Now what a lot of people don't understand is that running commercial training projects and operating outside of a regular military or government structure is very different. For a start always remember, if things go bad for whatever reason, you have no support. Your local embassies with do the minimum they are required to do if it gets to the stage of where you need their assistance.

Now one of the big issues that a lot of inexperienced trainers have is that they expect living conditions in a developing country to be the same as they are in U.S. or Western Europe. On one job in Mexico when we were staying in a police barracks my associate had a scorpion nest in his room and I had a rat in mine, we had be careful when leaving our rooms to make sure the free roving Rockweilers had been chained up.

Things that people take for granted like power, internet and gyms maybe limited or no-existent. While I was working in West Africa mains electricity could be on for maybe a couple of hours a day, so laptops were always plugged in, phones charged at every opportunity. In most places internet is available to some extent, so you need to see how the locals get it and make sure you're not getting scammed on rates. Food can be another issue for some trainers, don't expect steak, potatoes and doughnuts. If trainers and operators are fussy eaters or germaphobic it raises a red flag for me. To be able to operate in an environment you need to be comfortable in that environment!

Now a lot of training programs change because the facilities and equipment that was requested or expected are not available, so you have to work with what you have. In locations where there are issues with corruption you can expect problems with equipment being stolen or sold; on one job I ended up cutting a deal with a team leader of a tactical team on ammunition, as the allocation kept getting smaller without anything being shot. I understood their situation and my main concern was improving operational effectiveness of the team and for this I needed the co-operation of the team leader and the team members.

On the other end of the scale we once had a group attend a custom course we organized for them in Serbia. This group included two American instructors who had law enforcement backgrounds... This group stayed in the most expensive hotel in Belgrade and were the only people we had ever complain about the facilities we use in Serbia. In America the ranges are better, in America we bought new Glocks for the students, in America... These supposed experienced instructors were ignorant prima donnas that did not know the rest of the world is not like America!! In America tactical equipment, guns and ammunition are freely available and quite cheap, not so in most other countries.

I am lucky that over the years I have had some good guides and I remember one from when I was in South Africa in 94 made it clear to me you must respect and understand other cultures. He was white and of a British Army background and it was clear to me that his native employees respected him greatly. He told me he made it clear to his guys that some aspects of their culture he disliked, and their food disgusted him as he knew some aspects of his culture etc. disgusted them. But, he also made it clear he respected their culture and expected the same in return. It worked!

I have had to deal with various problems over the years that have voodoo and magic. Now for some this may seem a joke but in a lot of places voodoo and magic are part of the culture. One story I tell happened while I was working in Nigeria. A laptop computer went missing form a room at the training location and the trainees were the suspects. I was training about 60 vigilantes from 5 districts, many of whom could not read or write but this did not mean they were stupid! The next morning after the admin staff made a stink about the theft and the district leaders came to and told me they needed a few hours off to go and see who stole the laptop, they wanted to go and see the traditional doctor, the magic man! To turn them down would have been a slap in the face for them, they were going to spend money and effort trying to find who stole the laptop and it was their way of solving the problem. So, everyone wrote their name on a piece of paper and off they went to traditional doctor.

A few hours later they returned and told me they had found out who had taken the laptop, four ceremonies had been done and the same name had come up as the thief in all of them, it was the security guard for the buildings. The person running the program was American and had issues about firing the guard, who I wanted out of there ASAP! When the guard's bags were searched a mobile phone charger that one of the locals I was using as an instructor had lost a week or so before. This resulted in my instructor grabbing the guard's dagger and trying to stab him, luckily for the guard someone grabbed the blade before it hit him, which still resulted in a mess and a fair bit of chaos anyway. Needless to say, the guard was fired and left the compound pretty quickly. The laptop was never found but did the magic ceremonies identify the thief? Who knows, it's not my culture but I respect it!

How you behave is extremely important, people seem to forget that when on training and operational projects those that hired you will be watching you closely. For some, receiving attention and being treated by locals as a novelty can go to their heads, to say the least, which can result in problems especially when the novelty factor wears off. Big problems can arise when people make statements about politics or the performances of local police or military commanders etc. and start stepping on people's toes. Many instructors seem to forget that they are guests and that the local order of things will always need to be respected, even if it's to your liking.

As anyone who pays attention to what is happening in the international security world would have seen the U.S. secret service has been having numerous problems over the past few years with their people being caught up in stupid situations with prostitutes and getting publicly intoxicated. On long term jobs people need to let off steam, just do so in private and in a safe environment with trusted people.

It never ceases to amaze me how many men get their selves into trouble over women and this applies on operation and training projects also. Getting involved with local women can be a serious breach of security; again, just like the U.S. secret service agents in Cartagena, Colombia who were stupid enough to take the girls to their hotel rooms. There are plenty of "by the hour" hotels in Colombia, their brains should have been used in conjunction with their penises! In some places women can be provided by the clients, how you deal with such gifts will depend on your personal circumstances, refusal can lead to some awkward questions but if you accept always remember to tip...

The general rules for behavior should be that you want to be as anonymous as possible, show maximum courtesy to your clients and always respect the local culture and bureaucracy. Also knowing the local laws and limits of your responsibility is extremely important. Back stabbing and jealously exists in all aspects of the security business and sources of this need to be identified. In locations where there is a lot of internal bureaucratic power struggles going on people will be looking to trip up your project just to belittle those who contracted you for the job. On one job in Mexico we were called to meet the local police commissioner who told us he did not want us there, we were brought in by his superior without his knowledge.

One incident I had while working with the vigilantes in Nigeria resulted in a Mexican standoff between us and the army. The army and police chiefs for the area were informed there would be armed vigilante patrols operating but, within minutes of us hitting a paved road army patrols appeared wanting to confiscate firearms and make arrests. The vigilantes are community security teams where the army and police are federal organizations and have a greater authority. I understand this was a part of the local power struggle and the soldiers were just hoping for bribes. We had anticipated this problem but what complicated and infuriated me was that the person in charge of the project, who had met with the police and army chiefs and who we had on standby was delayed in getting to our location; because he was hungry and sent his driver to get beer and food, he ended up getting a taxi!! Never expect those in the rear to realize or want to get involved in the issues that can arise in the field, even if they can talk a good war, don't expect them to get their boots dirty!

Now to me the actual training of the students is the easy part of a training contract, hopefully you can see just getting to day one of the course can take a lot of planning and politics. Now when it comes to training the students you need to clarify what they really want and how hard they want to be trained. You may think that if people are paying for a training course they want to be trained to the max, not always so. When working in Latin America and Africa the students tend to want to be pushed hard and learn as much as they can. In the U.S. and Europe people tend to expect coffee, lunch breaks and to work a 9 to 5. This is where you need to work with the clients and see how they want training, they are the ones paying the bills. It used to frustrate me that if students did not want to train hard then they were not serious and not going to be up to a decent standard. These days I see it as their choice, as long as they are happy, and I get paid I am happy. I remember taking one individual in Florida for a private pistol class and this guy was shooting poorly even though he had a very expensive firearm. When I tried to correct him, he kept telling me that he had always shot the way he was shooting and did not listen to my advice. If people want to pay me and not listen to my advice that's their choice, you can't educate pork, but if they pay cash I am happy!

Now to me there is a big difference between lectures and training courses, something's you cannot teach solely by showing power point presentations and videos. It makes me laugh that a lot of close protection courses, especially in the U.S. are made up of nothing more that lectures, BS exercises in parking lots, some basic shooting and maybe a controlled trip to a restaurant. With our civilian courses our students run realistic exercises and on our Government courses the exercise where possible are live. This is best way for people to learn and also exposes them to some of the potential problems and stress of live operations.

On the larger training contracts, the student instructor ratios can be high as there is not the budget for more than a couple of instructors. When working with the vigilantes in Nigeria I usually had 60 students for 12 days courses. Initially I had to delegate to the district leaders to organize their people until I could select guys I could use as instructors. Those I tended to choose were those who generally had the most punishments during their courses and took it with a smile. It's easy to teach techniques to intelligent people but finding intelligent people who can take and give out punishment is another thing. Nigerian vigilantes tend to be a bit rough around the edges and need to be dealt with in ways they respect!

As I have said before you must always show respect to your clients and students. Some trainers have a superiority complex and seem to think that just because they are from a developed country that those from developing countries are stupid. This is a big problem and can lead to a lot of issues, especially when the trainers start to be shown up by their students. I have trained students over the years who were illiterate and not owned shoes but spoke multiple local dialects and could survive indefinitely in the bush with only a machete, skills I can only dream of having. In Latin America have worked with those that don't own a piece of brand name "tactical" equipment but understand the streets better than the criminals they deal with every day. I respect my students and over the years have learn a lot from them.

If you do not have your students respect then you are going to have problems, if you cannot do or have no operational experience at doing what you are teaching, then how can you expect your students to respect you. There are many instructors who are purely instructors and know what they have been taught and read, but no nothing of the problems of applying these theories on operations. As there are many students who have plenty of operational experience but never received any formal training. They know BS when they hear it because they already know what works and what does not work, that why they are still alive.

I have dealt with tactical teams trained by the British, French, Americans and even the North Koreans and what is always lacking are the basics. Everyone seems to want to show the high-speed entry techniques but forget about the basics like how to read a compass and approach a target location without detection. I remember one Mexican team who had received several months training from French and U.S. agencies, they looked pretty stacking up outside of a door, but had no procedures for dealing with offensive actions by the criminals. So, they were being taught procedures from countries where the criminals are very tame and compliant and then trying to employ these procedures against very aggressive, motivated and trained drug cartels... Things were not working for them... Again, you must understand the environment and opposition you will be training the students to deal with.

I like to identify the general fears of those I am training and exploit them; be it swimming rivers in the dark or standing between targets during live fire drills. This exposes the real character of the students and applies stress into the training, which is essential when training those who will be working in high risk areas. Safety must always be considered, but in my opinion in places like the U.S. and Europe people are more worried about a student breaking a nail that being operationally effective. When training serious students who will be using the skills taught, they tend to understand cuts and bruises go with the turf.

When running intense courses for government agencies in high risk locations we train the students hard; long hours, minimum breaks for food and constant activity. I am not one for the "positive re-enforcement" method of training, where even if people a screwing up they get told how good they are. This is used in a lot of U.S. law enforcement training and theory behind this is that the cop just needs the confidence to deal with the situation even if they are not that competent. This is acceptable in low risk locations like the U.S. and Western Europe, but when dealing with serious criminals I would want to be working with people that are competent and not those who just think they are competent; there is a big difference!

On all my courses I like my students to make mistakes and to take them outside of their comfort zones; anyone can talk like perfect tactical guy in Starbucks.

Students learn more from making mistakes and this also helps them see what they have been doing wrong. I tell my students if far better to make the mistakes during training rather than on operations. I have come across some that cannot handle having their faults identified and constructive criticism, this is just ego and insecurity issues on their part. I remember one operation that was carried out by the vigilantes in Nigeria that was a complete fiasco and I am glad to say it was nothing to do with me. They had good intelligence that several known kidnappers were staying in a village, a reconnaissance was done, and identities were confirmed. The operation was run by the area coordinator for the vigilantes who had no training and would not go through my courses. He gathered a group about 30 vigilantes and drove straight to the village with the vehicles sirens blazing, just like the movies. Needless to say, the kidnappers escaped and the guys I had trained were disillusioned with the coordinators actions. This operation was outside of my limit of responsibility anyway, but sometimes it's funny to sit back and let people show their true worth!

The first time we worked in Mexico we were training a state police tactical team and to say they had attitude and ego issues would be an understatement. After about 3-days straight training, one of their guys ending up in hospital and the team commander nearly being accidently shot by one of the team members they began to listen. They were another team that had be shown room entry techniques etc. but never trained to work as a team and had no discipline. We were with them 16 days and by the end they were a very effective team, maybe too effective.

Discipline is something that many people are lacking and is something that cannot be installed by lectures. There has to be consequences for incompetence and punishing the whole group for one person's stupidity usually leads to the group educating the wrong doer. Outside of the U.S. and Western Europe fighting and violence during courses is a lot more common, especially when the students are tired, hungry etc. Discipline needs to be enforced and, in some situations, it can quickly lead violence, this again goes with the turf.

Problem students need to be identified and if they are not able to comply with the program then they need to be dismissed. This can lead to issues if the dismissed student has influential friends and then the politics begins. In such situations my usual compromise for the dismissed student to be let back on the program is for them to complete a tasking that will take them outside of their comfort zone.

Hopefully you can see from this chapter that there is more to running a training program than just teaching lessons. The main problems come from the organization, planning and politics involved. Providing commercial training and operational service is a lot different than working for a government agency or military. You have to take a lot more things into consideration as for a start you have little or no real support network. You need to understand the culture and politics of those you're training. And most importantly, you need to get paid!

Considerations for Self-Defense
Fundamentals of Close Combat

- **Pre-Defined Strategy:** You must have a thought-out defensive strategy for dealing with potentially hostile situations
- **Maximum Use of Distractions:** You must make the maximum use of distraction to give you the fractions of a second you need to get to your weapon or initiate a strike.
- **Weapon Deployment:** If you can get to your weapon then why have it... If you can't set up the strike, then what have you been training for?
- **Head Shots/Throat Cuts or Strikes:** If you shoot, then shoot to kill... If you cut or strike, then end it quickly!

Firstly, you cannot learn how to defend yourself by reading a manual or sitting down watching DVD's, you have to go and practice. Here I will give you some pointers on what skills you need to develop to be able to defend yourself, and your families without using firearms.

There are many myths and schools of thought on what makes an effective unarmed combat or martial arts systems for real world self-defense. All I will say is that there are many people confusing martial art systems that are developed for sports fighting and hobbies as realistic self-defense systems. I have had students come through my courses that have been taught and trust techniques that work in a gym with a compliant partner but don't work in my classes where those they are training with are not so compliant. On the street trying to do a fancy technique on a criminal who will not be compliant, possibly on drugs or drunk and who will not be fighting fair can get you severely hurt to say the least!

Use of force is a last resort and should be avoided at all costs, fighting is for amateurs, if you do get into a situation where you must use force you want to end it quickly, not roll around on the floor and try to make your opponent tap out. As with everything else you must work out a plan of action and a strategy for dealing with a potentially violent situation. You must keep things simple, if a self-defense technique is difficult and complicated for you to master in a gym don't bother with it; on the street your only concern is doing damage to your opponent not worrying about your form.

Fights generally take place at very close quarters and, unlike the open space of a dojo or gym, there will be many obstacles which you can trip over or you can be pushed into. You will not have the space to get into a guard position or to do a textbook kick. Try kicking someone and then remain standing on the wet, tiled bathroom floor of a club or restaurant!

The main things you will need to win a fight are confidence and aggression, some people naturally have these qualities, and others don't. The armed forces instill these qualities into individuals through strenuous training, discipline, pushing people to their limits, physical and verbal abuse. They are difficult qualities to really teach people, especially civilians who might only attend a couple of one-hour classes a week. You need to realistically think about how you would handle being in a confrontation, not in a dojo or gym, but being attacked by some thug in some dark, side street who is going to stab you to death or rape you and then laugh about it. Visualize this situation and determine how you would genuinely feel and determine how you would be able to successfully defend yourself.

You also need some degree of physical fitness; by fitness I don't mean you need to be physically big or muscular and be of an Olympic standard. I have come across numerous well-muscled and big guys who, at first glance, would appear to be intimidating but when tested, could not fight. This may have been due to their lack of confidence and aggression or the fact they were just too big and slow. You need the physical ability to move, throw multiple punches and low kicks, remember, the more physically fit you are, the better fighter you will be.

Attitude

Over the years I have had students come to my classes who have been through other programs and told how they can prevent themselves being victimized and how as a potential victim they could defend themselves. To me these people were already being placed at a severe disadvantage by being told they were a potential victim, you're only a victim if you let yourself be. You need a positive attitude, why should you be afraid of some scum bag that tries to intimidate, bully and rob people for a living.

What a lot of people forget is that when a criminal is going to commit a crime they are going to be scared; they are breaking the law and can get arrested, beaten up or shot in the process. As I have said before criminals look for easy targets, they don't want problems as they are bad for business. Remember if you are going to be scared and nervous so are your attackers. Your attitude needs to be that with the knowledge and ability you have you can screw up anyone who wants to mess with you or your family. The criminal made the mistake of starting the fight with you and they are going to get broken up, that's it!

Strategies

To me this is the most important thing that you will need to consider when putting together a self-defense program. The criminals will have at least put together a mental plan and strategy for attacking you, so should you not have one for how to counter them? The easiest way to assess someone's personal security is to go up and ask them the time. Now think about how you would react if a stranger approached you and asked you the time; what's your body language going to be saying, are you going to tell them the time, will you be in a fighting stance, are there and obstacles in your area that can trip you up, can you access your weapons etc.

If you have already planned your reaction you're not going to panic, you'll just be going through your procedures and be setting the criminal up for a beating. So, if a stranger is approaching you start setting them up by assessing their body language, assessing your surroundings, getting yourself info a defensive stance, considering if you want your body language to be passive or aggressive, selecting target points on the stranger and how you'll be attacking them; by the time they are close to you, you are ready take them out at any time.

I tell my students when they are out and about on their daily business to always be considering how they could set up and attack those around them. The next time you are at the mall or in a coffee shop look at the biggest person in there and workout how you could drop them, go up to them and ask them the time and think about how easy it would be to take their knee out!

Body Language

One of the main things that you need to learn is how to assess someone's body language and control your own. This is very important in a self-defense situation as you need to try to identify someone's intentions and not telegraph to them your potential response.

There are three main components of communication between humans; spoken words contribute 7%, vocal tone and volume make up 38% and body language makes up 55% of the message. So, let's say you just meet someone at the local grocery store and they are telling you how they really like you and want to help you carry your bags to your car; while their breathing rate is shallow and accelerated, their sweating and making agitated movements with their hands, believe their body language and say no!

Start reading people's body language, at a basic level you can generally tell if people are happy, sad or angry. Even though it's not 100% reliable, someone's facial expressions are good indicators to what mental state the person is in. If someone is stressed, their faces will be flushed, they may be sweating, have veins protruding in their neck or forehead and they may be a tensing their facial muscles.

When you are out at the mall or in a restaurant or bar, watch the people around you and try to identify what mood they are in or what type of discussion they are having with others. It should be easy to identify if a man and a woman are on a romantic date or two business people are having a heated discussion, when in a coffee shop try to determine what people are looking at on their laptops; are they concentrating or goofing around. You must learn to read body language, because this will help you identify, avoid and if necessary react to potential threats.

Stress Reactions

When a person is involved in a stressful situation their body will undergo over 150 different physical stress reactions. These stress reactions will happen to you and criminals alike, you need to be aware of them and be able to notice them in yourself and others. A bodies stress reaction includes adrenal surges, increased heart rate and blood circulation, sweating, increased respiration, increased muscular tension, reduced peripheral field of vision, reduced decision-making ability and auditory exclusion.

If you have ever been involved in a car accident, try to remember how you felt just before, during and after then try to remember if you felt any of the above reactions. If you have ever tripped over something and subsequently fell, try to remember what it felt like; for example, did the time between you actually tripping and hitting the floor seem longer than the fraction of a second it took in actuality, were you sweating and was your heart beating rapidly when you hit the floor?

Learn to read your own body language as well as others, if you are in a situation and your heart rate starts to increase or you start to breathe quickly; try to identify why this is happening. This could be your body's sixth sense telling you that something is not right and to get ready to react to a hostile incident. Look for these stress reactions in people around you, if someone approaches you and their face is flushed, eyes are wide and bloodshot and have veins protruding in their forehead and neck, maybe you want to try to avoid them or be ready to put them down!

Warning signs that identify someone is agitated and a potential threat include direct prolonged eye contact, flushed face, accelerated breathing rate, sweating, veins in neck and forehead are protruding, fists clenching unclenching, hands moving towards a concealed weapon, hands rising getting ready to strike, head dropping forward to protect throat, eyes narrowing, looking to see if you are armed or at intended target's areas on your body, changing to side on shooting or fighting stance and lowering the body before launching an attack.

What I've described is someone squaring up to someone else; boxers do this before a fight to try to intimidate their opponent. When you see this in someone's body language get ready to defend yourself, get ready to move, get ready use your weapon or to break their knee and punch them in the throat.

Always remember, if the criminal is street wise they will be monitoring your body language and trying to predict your reactions. You should never give any indication that you are going to defend yourself, when you react it should be a total surprise to you attacker. If your strategy is to cry like a baby until the 6'3", 250 lb criminal is within your striking distance and then knee them in the balls and stick your thumb through their eye, I would say that sounds a lot better than squaring off with them and trying to get them in an arm bar!

From thirty years' experience of dealing with violent situations and training people of all genders and from all backgrounds, I have come to the conclusion that the easiest way to train people how to defend themselves is to teach them the weak spots on the body and how to attack them. There are numerous target areas on the body that only need to be attacked with nominal force to cause permanent if not lethal damage. In reality there is no way a 5'4" female who is 130 lb's will be able square off and successfully fight a 6'3", 250 lb male criminal, can the female break up the criminal, sure if they use the right strategy and forget about fighting fair. Remember, fighting is for amateurs, we want to avoid problems or end them!

Use of Force

The use of force is a last resort and you must do all you can to avoid confrontations. Unlike the movies, street fights are not glamorous and, if someone is hit over the head with a bottle they won't just shake it off and walk away unscathed. In reality, if someone is hit on the head with a glass bottle, there will be a lot of blood, someone will be going to the hospital and there is a very good chance in most places someone else will be arrested.

Even if you find yourself in a situation where you have the right to defend yourself, you must never use excessive force against the person who is attacking you. For example, if someone grabs your arm on the street and demands your wallet and you react by breaking his nose, who do you think would be in the wrong? The only evidence the police will have is your claim that the guy tried to rob you, and, if there were no other witnesses, it would only be your word against your attacker's. However, they will have the guy's broken nose as proof that you assaulted him.

In some countries the fact you are a foreigner and have struck a local could easily get you arrested, even if you were rightfully defending yourself. So, you must only use appropriate force when defending yourself and you must always be able to justify that the use of force was necessary. The laws on the use of force vary greatly from area to area, in places like the United Kingdom weapons are banned and if you hurt a criminal who was breaking into your home the chances are you'll be charged by the police; In Florida, U.S. if a criminal is breaking into your home and you are in fear for your safety you are within your rights to shoot them. Do your research, knowing the law is all part of an efficient self-defense program.

The Elements of a Counter Attack

Once you have identified that you are going to have to deal with a violent situation you need to quickly workout your strategy and put into operation your counter attack. There are three elements needed to win a confrontation; surprise, speed and aggression. If you can combine two of these elements in your counter attack, there is a greater chance you'll be successful.

- **Surprise:** This is the main thing that you require. Surprise will give you the edge in all confrontations, if the criminals don't expect you to attack them; they won't be ready to defend themselves.
- **Speed:** Your actions need to be fast and decisive, no hesitation!
- **Aggression:** Aggression will always beat fancy techniques.

Other things you will need to consider is what do you want your body language to say, are you close enough to hit the target areas on the criminal, are your standing on slippery or uneven ground, are there objects that can trip you up, look for objects you can use as weapons or that can provide you with cover.

Distractions

Distractions are very important in violent confrontations because they can give you the time needed to disable the attacker. For example, a man confronts you with a knife, he is three to four feet away from you. If you throw something at his head, such as your keys, wallet he will move, which gives you time to get close and take out his knee. A distraction could be throwing some coins, jacket or looking over the attacker's shoulder and pretending someone is there.

People eyes are drawn to distractions, when you are talking with someone take out your wallet or cell phone, hold it off to your side and move it around a little, the chances are the eyes of the person you're talking with will at some point be following the wallet or cell phone. Use this distraction in your strategies; if your approached by a criminal hold your wallet off to your left, when their eyes follow it kick them in the balls with your right foot, get the idea!

Improvised Weapons

The first rule of unarmed combat is to always pick up a weapon! Forget the Queensbury Rules and fair fighting, you must win and to win you have to fight dirty. Anything can be used as a weapon: pens, keys, glasses, plates, umbrellas, rolled-up newspapers, ash trays. Look around you and see what is close at hand and think how you could use it to defend yourself.

In some countries like United Kingdom, it is illegal to carry weapons of any description but if you know how to use everyday objects as weapons you will never be unarmed. When I am traveling I usually do not take any weapons with me, if I require something I'll find a local Wal-Mart or the like and head for the tool or kitchen section. Wherever you go make sure you comply with the local laws, the local police might let you off with using force to defend yourself but arrest and charge you for carrying an offensive weapon.

Ground Fighting

Do everything you can to avoid getting into a grappling match with an attacker and ending up on the floor. Ground fighting, MMA and wrestling techniques are for sports fighting and gyms. If you are in a street fight and end up on the floor you are in a potential lethal position, one good kick to your head can kill or cause you severe brain damage.

If you are taken to the floor, you should fight dirty, forget grappling techniques; go for eye gouges, ram you fingers up the attacker's nose, fish hook their cheeks, bite them and start breaking fingers. Try to get to your feet as quickly as possible, if your opponent is still on the floor when you are standing kick them just as they would kick you.

Striking Techniques

Punches, slaps and kicks are the most common techniques people use to defend themselves. Unlike the tough guys in the movies, do not rely upon one single strike to knock someone out and end a confrontation. There is a good chance that you may miss your target area, so you should attack a number of strike points all in succession. You should practice your striking techniques, even if it's by yourself and on an old punch bag. You must learn how to punch and kick properly, which does not take much time, punches and kicks thrown the wrong way can lead to injuries.

Here is list of some simple and effective striking techniques:

- **Closed Fist/Punch:** The conventional punch comes naturally and instinctively to most people. To form an effective fist, pull in your knuckles and thumb as tightly as possible and make sure your wrist is straight and locked. You want to be hitting you target with your knuckles, not your fingers. You can greatly increase the effectiveness of a punch by placing a pointed object such as a key, pen, coffee stirrer etc. between your fingers. Or keep your keys on a climbing carabineer, which can make a legal and very effective knuckle duster.
- **Fist Hammer:** The hammer fist can be an extremely powerful blow and there is a lower chance of injury to your hand. The hammer fist is formed just like a conventional fist for a punch, the difference is you hit the target with the sides of the fist. Again, the effectiveness of this strike can be greatly increased by adding and striking with a pointed object such as a pen.
- **Open Palm:** Striking with an open palm can carry the same impact as a punch; the main problem is if used incorrectly you will break your fingers and wrist. The important thing is to keep your thumbs and fingers locked in and not protruding. One of the main advantages of using open palm is that they portray passive body language unlike closed fists.
- **Bitch Slap:** Even if someone has problems performing a decent punch they can still bitch slap with some force. Simply cup the palm of the hand you are going to be hitting with and put it down by your side, then quickly turn your hips and bring the hand up to strike the side of the targets neck or head. This same strike can be done with the hammer fist.
- **Upward Knee:** This is a simple technique and at close quarters is a very powerful and effective. This technique is simply executed by raising and driving the knee into the target area.
- **Front Kick:** The front kick is a simple and effective technique; first raise your knee up, then extending your foot into to your target in one motion, your ground foot, the one you're not kicking with should be flat on the floor. Make sure the kicking foot is angled upwards and not pointed down, this is to prevent injuries to your ankle. Kicks can be a lot more powerful than punches and give you more range; also, if you are distracting the criminal with your hands they should not see the kick coming.
- **Stomp Kick:** This is a simple and very powerful kick that can do a lot of damage to an opponent's knees etc. Just bring up the leg up that you are going to kick with and come down as hard as possible on the target.

General Target Areas

Hitting these targets can cause permanent damage and, in several cases, possibly fatal results. These targets should only be used as a last resort where you are in fear for the safety of yourself and your family.

- Knees
- Groin
- Throat
- Eyes
- Fingers

Specific Target Areas

- **Forehead:** A good blow to the forehead can cause whiplash and a severe blow with an improvised weapon can cause a brain hemorrhage and death. The open palm is a good strike to this target as hitting this target with a closed fist could damage your hand.
- **Top of the head:** The skull is made up of plates of bone and there is a weak spot where the frontal cranial bones join. A strike to the top of the head with blunt weapons can causes trauma resulting in unconsciousness and death.
- **Temple:** The skull is weak at the temple and there is an artery and nerve just under the skin. A powerful strike with an improvised weapon or the knuckles of a closed fist can cause unconsciousness, concussion, if the artery is severed this will cause hemorrhaging and compression of the brain, which will lead to a coma and likely death. Hair: If you control the head, you control the body. If an attacker has hair then pull it as hard as possible, this will cause pain and can open up other target areas you can attack to end the situation.
- **Eyes:** The eyes are one of the main target areas you want to attack in a life or death situation, a finger jab can cause temporary blindness or with a more determined attack the eyes can be gouged out or ruptured. If a finger, thumb or a pointed weapon goes through the bone behind the eyes and into the brain it can result in the death of the attacker.
- **Ears:** A bitch slap with a cupped palm to the ear can rupture the eardrum and can cause a concussion. A ruptured eardrum is a very painful and possibly permanent injury. Ears can also be used to control the head, simply get a good grip of the attacker's ear and pull it. At very close quarters ears can be bitten, which can cause a lot of pain to your attacker.
- **Nose:** It does not take a very powerful blow to break a nose. Being hit in the nose causes pain, makes the eyes water and can produce a lot of blood. The theory that someone can be killed by driving their nose bone up into their brain is a myth, how many times do sports fighters break their noses and I have never heard of anyone being killed due to this. At close quarters a good technique is drive your fingers into an attacker's nostrils, this will cause a lot of pain and discomfort to your attacker and allow you to then target of points on their body.

- **Mouth:** I am a big fan of fish hooking for close quarters fighting. To fish hook an attacker you'll need to hook you finger or thumb inside of their cheek, get a good grip and pull in the direction you want their head to go. This technique is not very sanitary but is very effective and should be used in life threatening situations. A fish hook will cause the attacker a lot of pain and will allow you to access other target areas on their body to end the fight.
- **Jaw:** A strike from a closed fist, hammer fist or a blunt weapon to the jaw can dislocate or break it and cause unconsciousness.
- **Chin:** The open palm is a good technique to use on this target and can cause a concussion, unconsciousness and open up the throat for a lethal strike.
- **Throat:** A powerful punch or blow with an impact weapon to the front or throat can kill an attacker, it will at least cause extreme pain and gagging. A close quarter's technique is to grip and crush the windpipe which will lead to the death of the attacker.
- **Neck:** Any strikes to the front, side or back of the neck can cause pain and a jarring effect, powerful strikes and cause damage to the spine, hemorrhaging, unconsciousness and death. By driving you thumbs into the side of the neck or griping the neck muscles you can cause a lot of pain to an attacker.
- **Spine:** A power kick or blow with a blunt or edged weapon to the spinal column can result in paralysis or death.
- **Brest bone:** Even moderate blows to the breast bone with pointed objects such as a pen can cause severe pain; powerful blows can incapacitate an attacker.
- **Ribs:** A closed fist, kick or blow with a weapon are effective techniques against the ribs. The aim is to hit them hard enough to fracture them and drive them into the internal organs. Badly fractured ribs can cause damage to the liver, puncture and collapse a lung.
- **Back of hand:** The backs of the hands are full of small bones and nerves; striking this area can cause a lot of pain. A simple technique is that if someone grabs you stick a pen into the back of their hand, if the small bones on the back of the hand are broken the hand is ineffective.
- **Fingers & Thumbs:** Fingers and thumbs can easily be snapped which causes extreme pain. If you are forced to grapple or are grabbed by your opponent break their pinky fingers, keep hold of it and twist it. This will cause extreme pain to your attacker and get them to release their grip on you.
- **Groin:** Even a moderate blow to the groin of a male attacker and cause intense pain and put them out of a fight, powerful blows can cause unconsciousness and shock. A good punch, open palm, kicks or strike with an impact weapon will be effective against the target area.

- **Thigh:** A decent kick or strike with an impact weapon to the thigh can deaden the leg causing an attacker to lose his mobility or put them on the floor.
- **Hamstring:** A powerful kick or strike with an impact weapon to the hamstring can put an attackers leg out of commission; if the hamstring is cut, the leg is useless.
- **Knee:** Knee can easily be damaged or broken with a decent kick, in a serious confrontation this wants to be your first target on an attacker. A broken knee will cause an attacker a lot of pain, most probably permanent damage and put them out of the fight.
- **Foot:** The foot is made up of a lot of small bones that can be broken with a good stomp kick, this will cause your attacker a lot of pain. Also, if you stand on a person's foot and push them you should be able to put them on the floor as you are controlling their point of balance.

This chapter is only a basic guide to unarmed combat; unarmed combat cannot be learned from a book! Hopefully form this you can see you need to have a plan of action and strategy worked out, our best weapons are our brains and we need to use them, especially when involved in physical confrontations. You will have seen that some of the techniques I listed like eye and nose gouges, punches to the throat, fish hooks, finger breaks, are banned in Mixed Martial Arts and sports fighting systems. They are banned because they work, are easy to apply, can do permanent and possibly fatal damage to an attacker. If you are involved is a street fight you need to win, there is no referee there who is going to stop the fight if you're losing, you must do whatever is needed to win!

What's the Best Weapon: Knife or a Gun?

I am always being asked which is better for close quarters self-defense a gun or a knife. Both are deadly weapons if used properly but what is properly. At a close quarter's range, which is conversational range, say about 10 to 15 feet, the main thing will be if the weapons are deployed or not. Whichever one is deployed first gives the user the advantage. For the shooter at this distance you can forget the textbook formal line up the front sight shooting techniques, they won't work and for the person with the knife forget the Dojo sparing techniques. A lot would have to do with strategies, which seem never to be covered in formal firearms or self-defense training and then non-PC aggressive action!

Knives are excellent close quarter's weapons and have a lot of advantages over guns, like being legal availability in most places for one. If traveling internationally 98% of the time you can't take firearms but should be able to pick up a pocket knife at the end location. The tactical knife does not need to be a $200 + custom tactical blade, if you go to Wal-Mart you can get a paring knife that can be concealed and can slash and stab very well for under $10!

When dealing in Eastern Europe in the mid 90's I was surprised to hear from several law enforcement sources that the gypsy kids trained with knives, were skilled and were a not to be taken lightly. While in West Africa last year we were running all out tactical drills including hostage rescue with machetes, where the bush was thick it was very easy to stealthy get within a striking distance of a target. The proper use of knives relies on speed, surprise and aggression.

So, on the street for argument sake, who would have the advantage, the person with the knife or the gun?

- Whoever was not caught off guard to start with!
- Formally trained shooter against martial artists: Even!
- Street wise shooter against martial artists: The Gun!
- Formally trained shooter against someone who can use a knife properly: The knife!
- Street wise shooter against someone who can use a knife properly: Depends on the strategies, training and luck!

I tell my students and clients to do everything possible to avoid any hostile situation as there are no good end results... Someone usually goes to jail and someone usually goes to the hospital or the morgue!

First Aid Considerations

First aid is a subject which needs to be learned by everyone, first aid and CPR courses run the Red Cross and other recognized organizations are available in most areas for a small fee, if any. These courses will teach you the basics of first aid; if you are going to a remote of high-risk area you may need more in-depth training.

To work out what you need to know you first have to do a threat assessment on yourself, group and area you're going to. Things you need to consider are any known medical conditions you or your group members have, and do you know how to treat these conditions. Know what medications or drugs you or your group members are taking, and do they have a sufficient supply, or can they be obtained in the location you're visiting. Know what drugs you and other group members are allergic to and make sure to inform any medical staff of this in an emergency. Know everyone's blood type and whether the blood and needles in the local hospitals are sterile. Always know the exact location of local hospitals with emergency departments and if they accept your medical insurance or require cash before treating someone. Always know how to summon assistance and formulate an emergency evacuation plan.

When traveling internationally you need to be careful if you're carrying prescription drugs, keep the paper work with you to prove they were legally prescribed to you. It is good to know how to be able to put an IV-drip into someone but, in some countries, it is illegal to even possess the equipment, let alone use it without the appropriate certification. Always check with the embassy of a country you're visiting what medical equipment is illegal or legal to take with you.

You should always travel with some first aid equipment even though in most places, you will never be far away from a first aid kit. The quality of equipment in commercial first aid boxes can vary greatly and most will only be of use for dealing with very minor injuries. I put my first aid kits together myself and include some things that are commonly available, but most people would not consider for first aid. You should keep a well-stocked first aid kit in your residence and vehicle but for most people it would be impractical to carry a full first aid kit around with them at all times.

A basic improvised and highly portable first aid kit could consist of several Tampons, which can be used to plug cuts, gashes and puncture wounds; tampons are idea for this as they are made to absorb blood. Lengths of Gaffer Tape, which can be used to close wounds, stabilize broken bones with improvised splints and seal sucking chest wounds. I would also include some safety pins which can be used for stabilizing broken bones and put everything in a plastic zip lock bag. The plastic bag itself can be used for treating sucking chest wounds or for covering burns etc. You could do more with this small improvised kit if you know how to use it than you can with a lot of large commercial first aid boxes.

Another small and very versatile first aid I have consists of two American military first field dressings which are light, compact and have multiple uses from treating large cuts or gunshot wounds to stabilizing broken limbs. They also usually come in plastic wrapping which has multiple uses. I also include lengths of Gaffer tape, safety pins, sterile wipes, band aids, a length of bungee cord for a tourniquet and Steri Strips that can be used like stitches to close cuts. As there is a threat from being infected by viruses such as HIV and hepatitis when giving first aid, it is important to include protective equipment for when you're administering first aid. I include rubber gloves dealing with blood and body fluids and a protective mouthpiece for giving mouth-to-mouth resuscitation. This kit can fit into a small pouch or zip lock bag. I tend not to include any drugs in my first aid kits, if you are including drugs make sure they are legal at your destination and that they are not given to anyone who is allergic to them.

These two first aid kits can be put together quite cheaply, there is no need to spend hundreds of dollars on equipment. If you are traveling to an area where there is a potential threat everyone in your group should be carrying their own first aid kit in a location that is known to everyone else. That's because in the case of an emergency you can use their kit on them, you don't want to use your kit on someone and then have nothing left to treat yourself in an emergency. Your job will be to provide first aid and get the casualty to a doctor or hospital as quickly as possible, so you need not be too concerned about cleaning serious wounds, just keep the person alive so the doctors can deal with them.

Before you attempt to give anyone else first aid make sure it is safe for you to do so, never put yourself at risk. This might seem like a cold-hearted way to look at things but it's better that only one person is seriously hurt than two. This is a special concern when you are in potentially hostile environments where the opposition could be using the casualty to draw you in to their kill zone. You must always search the area around the casualty for potential threats and if you feel that is not safe for you to give first aid to the casualty, then don't. If you are operating with a team, somebody should stand watch and cover the personnel who are giving the casualty first aid. If you are your own remain aware of your environment and regularly check your surroundings for potential threats. Your safety always comes first!

Basic First Aid Tips

- Assess the casualty and treat in the following order: Breathing, Bleeding, Breaks, Burns,
- Cardiopulmonary resuscitation (CPR): If someone is not breathing you need to remove any obstructions from the mouth or throat, open their airway, pinch the casualty's nose closed to prevent air escaping, take a full breath and place your lips around the casualty's mouth and make a good seal, blow into the mouth until the chest rises, repeat breath and assess casualty, check pulse and look for signs of recovery, if there is a pulse keep breathing for the casualty and assessing the recovery signs.
- If there is no pulse in the carotid artery in the neck for 10 seconds, place your hands on the casualties chest and place the index finger of your lower hand over the point where the lower ribs meet the breastbone, place the heel of your other hand on the breastbone; slide it down to meet your index finger, place the heel of your first hand on top of the other hand and interlock the fingers, when giving chest compressions lean well over the casualty and keep your arms straight, press down vertically on the breastbone and depress it by about 4 to 5 cm. You'll need to complete 30 chest compressions at a rate of 80 to 100 a minute and give two breaths of mouth to mouth, continue until help arrives
- If a person is bleeding from a wound you should lie them down, raise the limb as high as you can and try to control bleeding by pressure points, apply a dressing by pressing down firmly over the wound, cover the wound completely with dressings and bind them firmly into place, If the bleeding will not stop, apply more dressings and bind them tightly, do not remove the blood soaked dressings.
- To stop infection in minor wounds, remove and foreign matter and clean them with regular soap and hot water.
- If someone has severed an artery and blood is spurting from a wound applying dressings and elevation will not stop the bleeding. You will need to apply a tourniquet; these can be improvised from a belt or piece of clothing. Put the tourniquet around the cut limb four inches above the wound and tighten it by twisting a stick or pencil slipped through the tourniquet knot. Once blood flow is controlled, tie the stick into place. You'll need to loosen the tourniquet every 15 minutes to half hour to let blood flow into the injured limb to prevent it from dying and getting gangrenous.
- Puncture wounds to the lungs can cause a sucking chest wounds, these can be identified by blood bubbling around the wound and a hissing sound made when the casualty is breathing. These wounds are extremely dangerous as they can lead to collapsed lungs, which can be fatal. You need to seal a sucking chest wound with plastic sheet, foil or some other similar airtight material. The

plastic sheet will need to be taped down on 3 sides around the wound; the 4th side is left untapped to let air and blood escape. When the wound is sealed lie the casualty on their non-injured side and get them to a hospital ASAP.
- Cuts to the stomach are very difficult to deal with especially if the intestines are hanging out of the wound. Never try to push them back inside, all you can do is place a dressing over them to prevent further contamination and keep the dressing damp by pouring water over it. If the casualty is thirsty just let them suck on a wet cloth, do not give them anything to eat or drink. You'll need to get professional medical assistance ASAP!
- If the casualty has a broken arm or leg the limb should be immobilized by being splinted, pinned or tied tightly to their body and then taken quickly to a hospital.
- If someone has been burnt cool the burnt area with cool water or ice, remove any tight clothing and jewelry, cover the burn with a sterile dressing and keep assessing the casualty for indicators they are going into shock. Shock is an extremely dangerous condition that you always need to take into consideration when dealing with casualties and those who have been involved is stressful situations. Shock can be caused from someone suffering physical injuries or by psychological reactions to stressful situations. Someone goes into shock when the body's blood pressure drops to extremely low levels, this can result in death even though the casualty's injuries are not life threatening. Signs of shock include rapid shallow breathing, weak rapid pulse, pale blue skin especially around the lips, sweating, weakness and giddiness, nausea, gasping for air, mental confusion and loss of consciousness. To treat shock, lie the casualty down and loosen any tight clothing, maintain the casualty's body temperature at a reasonable level, reassure and keep the casualty calm, monitor their breathing and pulse rates.

This chapter is just a quick guide to a very detailed subject that cannot be learnt from reading a book. If you are an international traveler I would strongly suggest that you go and take some basic first aid and CPR classes, hopefully you'll never need them, but it always pays to be prepared for the worst.

Traveling with Guns & International Self-Defense

I am always being asked about which guns are best for close protection details and personal defense etc... My answer is whatever you have access to and what hopefully goes bang when you pull the trigger!! In the U.S. people are spoilt as far as firearms are concerned, in most U.S. states they are freely available to those without criminal records and the use of force laws are very lenient. This is not so in many other countries!

If you are traveling internationally the chances are you will not be able to take firearms with you due to the laws in the country you are visiting, which you need to check before travelling. In many countries you can take sporting/hunting guns if you manage to get a permit from the embassy of that country before you travel. This can be a long and difficult process and will also put yourself and your project on the radar of the country you're visiting before you even get there. If you get permission to take a firearm with you into another country the chances are the permit will not be carry permits. In most places citizens and legal residents of that country are the only ones who can get firearms ownership permits and carry permits, if they are available.

It is also very important know the laws on use of force and restrictions on any weapons such as knives and pepper spray you may want to carry. In places such as England if you caught with the type of pepper spray you can buy at a gas station in most of the U.S. your looking at being arrested and I believe spending up to 2 years in prison.

Even in countries that have a reputation for high crime and violence the chances are that firearms will officially be regulated, usually strictly. I was recently asked to train a U.S. team who claimed to be going to Mexico, where firearms are very restricted, officially, even for Mexican citizens. When I asked these guys weather it they wanted an armed or unarmed course they said armed. When I asked them how they were going to carry in Mexico, they said they were working on it. More like dreaming, sure if you're working for the Cartels you'll get guns no problems, I hung up, I don't waste my time on such people.

I hear regularly of people that have armed contracts in Mexico and are looking for bodyguards etc. These people and companies are 99.9% of the time just looking to build a data base of resumes/CV or to promote themselves. I also hear stories of people claiming to work armed in Mexico, claiming to run hostage rescue missions etc. Well as I am writing this just yesterday a U.S. Marine, Sgt. Andrew Tahmooressi, was released from 8 months in a Mexican jail for accidently driving down a wrong border road and in to a Mexican police check point, with U.S. legal firearms in his vehicle. So, how do you think the Mexican Authorities would react to someone dressed in tactical gear with an AR-15 claiming to be there to do a hostage rescue mission. Well, if they did not get shot straight away they would be going straight to jail and being paraded for all the international news channels to see!

Reality check: In Mexico if you caught carrying a gun without the right paperwork, which is impossible to get for foreigners or non-Mexican military or police personnel you will have problems. If you are caught by the police or involved in a shooting you're going to jail and better have plenty of $$ available if you want to get out. If you're caught in a cartel road block and they find a gun... The best hope for you is they kill you quickly!! You may feel like a tough guy with a 9mm but up against half a dozen shooters with AK's and AR's you're going to have issues!!

Another recent example was of the crew of the U.S. Salvage Vessel the "Aqua Quest" who were arrested in Honduras and held for two months in Jail. Honduras is one of the most dangerous countries going but they still strictly enforce gun laws. In this case it seem the crew took in weapons that were not legal in the country, combine this with entrepreneurial police and you have a big problem. Both the crew of the "Aqua Quest" and "Sgt. Andrew Tahmooressi" were very lucky to get released but they had family and supporters who pushed the cases for their innocence. As a security contractor don't expect such niceties, you will be guilty until proven innocent. A good example of this is the four Blackwater guards that were recently convicted for multiple chargers in the case of the Baghdad shooting in 2007.

Most international protection jobs are unarmed; Iraq and Afghanistan are unique situations that I doubt we we'll see again. Close protection operators must know how to avoid problems, which is where the skill lies. I can teach someone to shoot in a day, to teach someone to be street wise and able to operate takes a lot longer.

When considering traveling with weapons you need to ask yourself some simple questions, as usual you're doing a threat assessment. You need to consider: 1) The legalities of carrying weapons and use of force? 2) Will you actually need to be armed? 3) What weapons are available? 4) The consequences if stopped by police or criminals? 5) The consequences for use of force?

1) **The Legalities of carrying weapons and use of force:** You need to know firstly if it is legal to import or carry firearms or other weapons. This where you need to do your research, contact the countries embassies or ask contacts within the country what the regulations are. Also, you need to know what the laws on the use of force are, as these vary greatly. In U.S. states such as Florida if someone threatens you with a knife and you are in fear for your safety you can shoot and kill them, no problems. In some South American countries, a knife is not seen as being the same threat level of a gun, so you would need to initially use impact weapons etc. to counter a knife attack! This may not seem logical to some but it's the law and you need to know it, especially if you have to deal with the police.

2) **Will you actually need to be armed:** The answer to this question most of the time in reality will be no! I have come across numerous people over the years who consider anything outside of Western Europe or the U.S. as a war zone. I have heard of people claiming to have turning down jobs in Africa, in places which are in reality safe and where I have partied because they could not carry a gun... I had one wealthy student and new resident to Miami Beach wanting to buy a .50 sniper rifle to shoot anyone stealing his motor yacht from the bottom of his garden, I take he watched "Scarface" a few to many times. He changed his mind when he realized there was a very good chance of him doing life in prison if he ever tried sniping a Miami Beach pirate, better just to insure the boat! Now, what if your assessment says yes you need to be armed but it's not legal to do so. Are you going to risk it or turn the job down, that is something only you can answer!

3) **What weapons are available:** Now, you have decided you need to be armed so where will you get the weapons from and what is available. As, I have said in a lot of countries only citizens of that country can buy firearms and it can be a lengthy process. So, if you cannot take a firearm with you can you borrow a firearm from a local contact and will it be legal? Can you by weapons on the street or black market and again is that legal? If you cannot get hold of firearms, then what else is available? If you are properly trained you can turn most things into some sort of impact or edged weapon. Now, if you can get firearms what are the best to have? My answer to this is what is reliable and what has a good supply of ammo and parts. I was working in South Africa in 1994 and was initially given a 4 inch .357 Taurus revolver that was rusted and as dry as a nun's crotch. Don't expect people to give you their best weapons, have to learn to use what you're given and to complain enough to get what you want. .357 revolvers are still a favored weapon of mine BTW!

4) **The consequences if stopped by police or criminals:** Now you have your pistol with you or your shotgun in the trunk of the car and you're stopped by the police, are there going to be any issues. Is your paperwork good, really good? Will it help if you pay a bribe or will that cause you more

problems? Even in Florida, U.S. where you can legally carry pistols etc. I regularly hear of people getting a hard time from the police because they are armed. One guard that was working for me was stopped by the police when going home from a detail one morning. The cops had him sat on the sidewalk as they searched his truck, he knew he had nothing to hide and it was quicker to consent to a search than wait for a K-9 to be called out. The guard had 3 State licenses so, why did the police do this, why not? I take it they were bored, saw the Blackwater sticker on his truck and wanted to mess with him. So, what if he was with a client... Same thing can happen, the cops if they see there is an opportunity to drop a business card to the client will mess with the guard; run a check the serial number of the gun, unload and strip it before returning it etc. And this is in a supposed first world country. Now, think about if you're stopped by Cartel in Central America, would you want to be carrying the Glock 17 which is an excellent weapon but screams Government issued or a small nickel plated snub revolver which just says you're a bit wise and carful... Consider all angles, the bad guys do!

5) **The consequences for use of force:** The biggest issue when carrying weapons is what are the ramifications if you must use them. Even if the use of force is justified you can initially be arrested and go to jail until the facts are sorted out. In countries where the police are entrepreneurial the fact a foreigner killed a local with open the opportunity for a potential pay day! One incident from South America; a businessman with a pistol carry permit was attack by a robber with a knife. The business man flashed his gun and the criminal backed off, only to attack again as the businessman was just entering his car. End result the criminal was killed, 100% justified defensive shooting. That shooting cost the businessman $20,000.00 not to go to jail for a long time. The police and the judge knew he had some money and now had an opportunity to extort him, this is how things work... $20K was a far better deal than going to a 3rd world jail! The other issue with killing people is that in a lot of places their families or fellow gang members will be coming after you and your family. I know of several cases where ex-pats had to leave Latin American/Caribbean countries because of personal safety reasons after they justifiably killed a bad guy.

I tell me students and clients that guns can get you out of trouble but can also get in you into a lot more trouble! If you're working armed, you need to have done your homework and worked out how you're going to deal with all the potential problems that can occur from carrying a weapon and using force etc. For example, if you drop someone are you going to hang around and possible end up in a 3rd world jail or go straight to plan "Foxtrot Oscar"? Most people in the close protection business see themselves as reactionary; if they are attacked they'll save their client... There is a bit more to it than that! Here's a tip, if your low profile and it gets to the stage your being attacked you've missed something and will most probably be the first to die, hopefully quickly!

Gun Addiction...
It could ruin you Masculinity!

Gun addiction is something I have seen numerous time over the years and from a tactical and security point of view can be a serious problem. I am not a big TV fan, but the other week was watching/listening to a survival show called "Alone" which, I think is on Discovery Channel. It has a good concept where ten men are stranded individually in locations on the Canadian coastal wilderness with some equipment, where they have to set up to live long term using their outdoors and survival skills. The challenge is to see who can last the longest living off the land.

What I found amusing and disturbing was that several of the competitors dropped out due to what they perceived to be aggressive wildlife (bears & wolves) and them not having a firearm. Okay, from a survival point of view; wildlife can be very dangerous in such places, but shouldn't these problems have been identified and contingencies planned? From a mindset point of view, in a survival situation I am going to be thinking how I can trap and eat these animals, if they come to me then it saves me having to find them. What did mankind do before guns, I don't think the Native Americans who lived in that area were living off veggie smoothies from their local Wholefoods store or calling an attorney when they had issues with bears taking a dump outside of their tents... This to me was an example of addiction to guns, the inability to operate without a firearm.

The above example is a bit extreme, but I have come across many people in the continental U.S. who also seem to be terrified at the thought of being without a firearm. For the records, I am very pro-gun and think everyone one should have the right to carry a firearm when they are properly trained to do so. But, guns are part of a security or survival plan not all there is to the plan!!

Another example came to mind and I give as an example on my courses. I was speaking with someone last year about security issues etc. And this person was former U.S. Military, law enforcement and a DOD contractor was telling me how he turned down a government job in Abuja, Nigeria because he could not carry a firearm; "Got to have a gun in Africa"! I think he was trying to impress me but I have spent time in Africa, mainly unarmed. I have been out partying in Abuja and worked there providing bomb prevention services to Churches, unarmed! Abuja is a pretty safe city as long as you're sensible, as with any major city, and is one of the safer places in Nigeria in general.

To put things into context, about the same time Mr. Tactical Ted was telling how he would not set foot outside the U.S. without a gun I had someone handing out terrorist attack and bomb prevention booklets to churches in volatile part of Nigeria. This someone was a young lady I knew, Ms. Jenny, who was a student at the time and a local beauty queen. There are numerous terrorist attacks in her area, the last a few weeks ago, but she was still traveling around distributing the booklets and she was unarmed. I am sure to Mr. Tactical Ted the distribution of these booklets would have needed an armored convoy with air support but. Things are different in the real world!

So, in the terms of basic self-confidence, composure and operational procedures who would you say rates the highest; Mr. Tactical Ted or Ms. Jenny? I think Ms. Jenny wins hands down, job done way before I expect Mr. Tactical Ted would have finished writing his kit list! While Mr. Tactical Ted would be thinking body armor and hollow points I am sure Ms. Jenny was thinking would her nail varnish match her shoes and handbags.

Guns have an application in a security program, but many people seem hooked to the belief that all there is to self-defense and close protection is having a gun. Most places in the world, including 99% high crime countries, are very restrictive on firearms and as a visitor you are not going to get legal permission to carry or possess a firearm. It is also a fact that street criminals in high crime areas are very good at what they do, so I would say the majority of those carrying firearms for self-defense would end up dead pretty quickly if all they are relying on is their target shooting skills. Fact: You must be able to defend yourself without total reliance on firearms.

When I am on shooting ranges, including nice air-conditioned indoor ranges, and see shooters, including instructors dressed up with plate carries, chest rigs, daggers and drop holsters trying to look as mean as their YouTube heroes I find it pretty worrisome. I know for a fact many of these guys never joined the military for whatever reason, I expect most have never been in a bar fight let alone in a high-risk country, but they seem addicted the tactical lifestyle. What are they trying to over compensate for, I am sure Viagra would be cheaper that the thousands of dollars of guns and gear they walk around in.

Maybe they need to take some tips from someone who has operated successfully in a high-risk area like Ms. Jenny, I think most would be happier! Instead of worrying about the speed of their magazine changes she could teach them to be confident in how to properly apply their makeup... Instead of stressing about a new holster for their new gun she could boost their self-worth by ensuring their high-heels always matched their handbags... Maybe they would become empowered enough that armed with their new skills and wardrobe they could occasionally leave their guns at home....

So, if they are legally available learn to use and include firearms in your security and survival plans but also have other options available. I understand for many that gun addiction is a serious issue, but it does nothing but gives you a false confidence and security... And when the guns are not there it can result in extreme anxiety and panic for the addict... The best way to avoid any addiction is education, so learn other options to avoid or deal with hostile situations...!

Tactical Gear List & Considerations for SHTF

I am asked regularly what equipment people should have or need for tactical or hostile situations. I am not a gear-queer and tell people to make maximum use of what they have in their everyday environment, there is no need for camouflage knife, forks, and spoons. I am a great believer in the saying that "The more you know, the less you need" and I tell my students always look for equipment that is multi-use or think how something can be adapted for multiple uses.

Let me ask you a question... What makes equipment tactical? For me all that makes equipment tactical is the word "Tactical" which, is overly used these days by stores and manufactures to sell Chinese made junk. Apart from firearms and ammunition a lot of useful equipment can be found in most hardware or kitchen stores. The advantage of kit from hardware or kitchen stores is that it's meant to be used and worked with, not just talked about, and played with as is the case with a lot of tacticool kit. For example, I always buy my flashlights from hardware stores, they are generally a lot cheaper than tacticool flashlights and take AA batteries etc. that are more widely available than fancy lithium batteries. From a tactical perspective, you don't need powerful flashlights, they need to be powerful enough for the job, you want to see, not be seen!

Camouflage and tactical black kit may look cool when you are showing it off to your buddies but, try finding the camo flashlight or zippo you dropped in the bush when you need it... As, long as kit does not shine or reflect light it will be fine. When buying, equipment think about if you drop it, which you will, would it be easy to find! In potentially hostile environments all but essential equipment needs to be packed or in your pouches or pockets, so your orange spork, which would be easy to find if dropped, should not be tucked in your hat band!

The below personal tactical equipment list is taken from a proposal I put together for counterinsurgency / tactical team in West Africa a few years ago, this should give you a few hints on kit etc. I have made some explanations on why I have included some of the items, and not every item will be applicable to everyone in every situation, so use this as a guide and adapt it. This is a tactical kit list for operational personnel and I am sure some reading this will say it's not applicable for most security or close protection personnel etc. OK, then don't read it, but remember not so long-ago Libya, Syria and The Donbass (Eastern Ukraine) were peaceable countries, whose populations would not have believed you if you told them civil wars would tear them apart. All of these are areas where close protection services are required.

From a U.S perspective look at what happened in New Orleans with hurricane Katrina in 2005 or the situation in South Chicago. Not so far afield look at what's happening in Mexico, could this happen in the U.S., to an extent yes... The Mexican Cartels in the U.S. generally keep things amongst their own communities, they are making plenty of money and compared to Mexico they are relatively safe. But with the strengthening of security on the U.S./Mexican border, which will lead to human and drug trafficking routes being cut, things could spill over. What trafficking routes are left will be fought over and the now unemployed narcos will be seeking other sources of income.

Such situations can lead to what can be classed as "Bosnification". Now when society breaks down, who takes charge? Sadly, in most places its usually the organized criminals; they are organized, armed and willing to take risks. After the Soviet Union collapsed Mafia groups took control in one way or another of local governments throughout the former USSR. Many of the irregular units fighting in the civil wars in the Balkans in the 1990's were formed by what could be classed as Mafia bosses. You can see it these days in Iraq, Libya and Syria where local militias have taken control of areas and change sides on a regular basis, and in the meantime the local populations have to deal with their BS and taxes.

In Mexico, in theory, there is the Military, Federal Police, State, and Municipal Police to enforce the laws but much of the country is controlled by drug Cartels and their offshoots. I have worked in Mexico and the police there have an extremely difficult job. I have trained some very effective police tactical units in Mexico who in the long run were disbanded or became ineffective due to being targeted by criminals. State and local police generally live in the areas they work in, if not from and grown up in those areas, which makes it easy for the Cartels to identify them and their families. Even if the officers want to do their jobs properly are they going to put their families lives at risk to do so, or just take their pay check and look the other way. In many situations where regular law and order has broken down, be it in Mexico or elsewhere it has been up to the local communities to protect themselves.

Now, when considering what equipment, you need put it into four different layers and think what gear you need, rather than what you want. I have use British Army Infantry terminology to help explain this section, each layer would be added on as required.

- **Personal Items:** Think about what should be on your person and at hand at all the time; knife, pistol, pistol magazines, cell phone/radio, lighter, personal water filter, basic first aid kit.
- **Assault Order:** This would consist of the essential kit needed to conduct a short-term military type tasking in a potentially hostile environment; rifle, spare magazines, water bottles, comprehensive first aid kit, protective clothing etc.
- **Combat Order:** This is the Assault Order with rations and personal equipment, that enable the you to live and fight for a period of 24 hours.
- **Marching Order:** This is the Combat Order with the addition of a field equipment such as backpack, sleeping bag, poncho, cooking stove, spare socks etc. required for two week operations without resupply, except for ammunition, rations, and water.

As I stated earlier this kit list was put together for a government team who had access to military weapons, I know in most places civilians will not be able to get AK's and CS grenades, so make use of what you have. If all I had access to was a double barred shotgun I would be happy, it's a very effective weapon if you know how to use it and have your strategies planned! If you have access to firearms buy weapons that you can get spare parts and magazines for, in common calibers. I have heard people applauding the FN 5.7 as the best pistol on the market, and I will admit it's a very nice weapon, but trying to get the ammo at the best of times can be a pain, during a SHTF situation, it might be easier to find rocking horse shit... I would suggest you stick to 9mm, .40 or .45 etc...

Team Formation & Equipment

Team operatives need to be carefully selected not only for physical abilities but also for social skills and their ability to bend in with other people. This means the best operatives are usually average height and weight and look like normal people. The operatives need to be physically fit and should be trained in light infantry tactics, first aid, communications etc. The operatives will need a high standard of self-discipline and intelligence; they will need to be mentally flexible enough to adapt to rapidly changing situations. The operators will need to be able to work by themselves or in team with minimal equipment and support. Our suggested size for an operational team is six operatives, this size team should be able to handle most tasks and be able to be split into two three-man independent fire teams. The team should consist of a team leader, a second in command and four operatives.

Equipment

The operatives need to be able to operate with minimal equipment and be able to adapt everyday objects to meet their needs. The operatives should be as lightly equipped as possible, too much kit will only slow them down. When on operations they should only carry what is necessary, if they don't need it, don't carry it. Below is a list of equipment the operative should have access to for cover and overt operations, they will not need everything for every operation.

Personal Equipment

1. Communications; Radios, cell/mobile phones. *Note: Consider if the cell phone networks will be working in SHTF situations. Remember with radios, the more powerful they are the easier they are to intercept from a distance. Make maximum use of smart phone apps if they do not compromise operational security. All communications equipment needs to be secured at all times.*
2. Power; mobile power sources need to be available for charging communication devices etc. Consider solar options.
3. A reliable wrist watch
4. Two good quality high capacity pistols with minimum of 6 magazines: We recommend two identical full-size service weapons.
5. Concealable/duty pistol holsters; strong side and shoulder rigs.
6. One folding stock rifle/carbine with minimum 6 magazines. We recommend AK-47 type platforms. *Note: AK platform was chosen for this location due to availability, always chose weapons you can get spare parts and ammunition for.*
7. Chest rig capable of holding 6 rifle magazines and two water bottles
8. Plenty of ammunition for operations and training.
9. Weapon cleaning kit
10. Waterproof flashlight and batteries
11. Personal first aid equipment
12. A quality fixed blade knife
13. Quality multi-pliers
14. Quality pruning shears/secateurs. *Note: used for building hides and clearing trails of brush that can make noise etc.*
15. A quality compass, Maps of operational areas, GPS with software updates.
16. Minimum two 1 liter water bottles, water purification tablets or personal filters.
17. A level 3A concealable bullet proof vest. *Note: protective clothing does not want to inhibit movement and remember the heat factor!*
18. Smoke/CS grenades. *Note: In previous articles I have mentioned from a civilian perspective smoke dischargers are used for maritime distress signals and available at most boat supply stores. Also, paintball/airsoft players use smoke in milsim games, they seem to have a wide selection available online etc.*
19. Two Carabiners & 20 meters of 9.2 mm climbing rope
20. Scrim net/sniper veil
21. Backpack, poncho, sleeping bag, stove etc.

Team Equipment

1. Spotting scopes
2. Night vision
3. Stills and videos cameras
4. Bolt cutters/entry tools

Dress

Operatives should dress to blend in with their environments; civilian cloths should be used for tactical operations especially when working in close proximity of civilians. A simple green or brown shirt can blend in to bush just as well as camouflage if the operative is properly trained. Our preference for civilian cloths over military fatigues is because if you are performing an operation in a suburban/urban area you have to blend in with the public and if you are wondering around the streets in military fatigues and face paint you will draw attention.

For footwear, we suggest to wear what the general population is wearing, something light that is good for running and swimming in. Tactical boots can draw attention and their aggressive tread leave obvious ground sign. If using running shoes, ensure any reflective material is removed.

The only specialist clothing we would recommend would be a fire proof balaclava and gloves. The balaclava can be used for concealing your identity and hiding the shine from your face on rural operations. Good gloves amongst other things gives you extra grip on your weapon and again hides the shine from your hands on rural operations etc. Tactical cloths for direct action operations should be fire proof and of a good quality.

Cash

Cash and assets will need to be available for operational expenses and to pay sources for information or services provided. Operatives should sign for all cash and assets and get recites or at least record all expenses.

Safe Houses

Teams and operatives will need places to work from, live and train. Locations will need to be secure and defendable. A threat assessment needs to be compiled on all locations uses by the team; weak spots must be identified and dealt with. Escape routes need to be identified from the safe houses to other safe locations or ERV's. All potential surveillance and sniper locations around the safe house need to be identified and monitored. Doors and windows on all floors need to be secured, reinforce or blocked if they are not used. The safe houses should regularly be searched for listening devices, cameras or IED's. When entering a safe house that has been left unoccupied even for a short period of time the whole place needs to be search for intruders, signs of intruders or forced entry. If a safe house is broken into it should not be used again. Fire alarms and firefighting equipment needs to be available and in working order. Above all the safe house does not want to draw attention; it needs to appear to be a normal house. It is difficult if not impossible to find the perfect safe house, find the best you can and take all precautions.

Transport

All vehicles used by the operatives needs to blend in with the environment they will be working in and not draw attention. When working in vehicles you should where manpower allows always have two operatives in a vehicle. One would be the drive, who should always stay in the vehicle, behind the wheel ready to drive away in an emergency and the other would act as escort or navigator. Windows where possible should be tinted for surveillance purposes. The vehicles should be registered to front companies and not to the operatives or the agency they are working for, so they cannot be traced back to you by the terrorists. Vehicles should be reliable and regularly serviced, all should have a good brake down kit. You will also need a recovery plan for immobilized vehicles and stranded personnel. When a vehicle is left unattended the area around it needs to be search and then the vehicle needs to be searched for IED's, tracking devices or contraband.

In urban areas, public transport should be used as it is good for identifying terrorist surveillance, losing anyone who has you under surveillance and is not usually an expected mode of transport for an operative.

Conclusion

Hopefully this article has given you a few things to think about. The main thing I try to stress to people about equipment is keep it simple and keep it to what you need... Remember, the more you know, the less you need!

Countering Snipers

I am sure there are those who initially looked at the title of this article dismissed it as something that will never apply to them and that it is just fear mongering. Personally, I think the information here is applicable to everyone who is working in hostile environments or with high-risk clients. Examples of high-profile sniper shoots include:

- Zoran Đinđić, the sixth Prime Minister of the Republic of Serbia, was assassinated on March 12, 2003, in Belgrade, Serbia. Đinđić was shot from approximately 180 meters away, using a 7.62mm Heckler & Koch G3 rifle as he exited his vehicle outside the Serbian government headquarters. He was shot in the heart and died almost instantly, his bodyguard was also seriously wounded in the stomach by another shot.
- Kurdish crime boss Aslan Usoyan was killed in a sniper attack in central Moscow on January 16th, 2013. The assassin used a silenced 'Val' 9mm assault rifle. One of Usoyan's bodyguards reportedly returned fire with several blind shots, but the fact that it took some time for police to find shooter's position showed that the bodyguard had failed completely at locating the sniper. Usoyan was shot in the head, a woman walking near the mob boss stepped into the assassin's firing line. According to LifeNews daily's timeline, the hitman attempted to move her by shooting her in the thigh. When she remained upright, she was shot again in the chest and fell, allowing the sniper to hit Usoyan once more as his bodyguards grouped around their wounded boss.
- Montenegrin gangster Dalibor Djuric was shot in the chest by a sniper on 22nd September 2016 while outdors in the yard of the Spuz state prison in the Montenegrin capital Podgorica. The jailed Mafia boss of one the rival drugs clans in the resort of Kotor was shot dead in prison while serving a two-year sentence for extortion. Police blocked the streets surrounding the Spuz prison to try to locate the assassin, but only found a car set on fire near the prison.
- Nicola Rizzuto was killed on November 10, 2010, he was the leader of the Sicilian faction of the Rizzuto crime family in Montreal, Quebec, Canada. Rizzuto was killed at his home when a single bullet from a sniper's rifle

which went through two layers of glass in the rear patio doors, the gunman was hiding in the woods outside the mafia boss's Montreal house.

Three of the above assasinations were of Mafia bosses, and I am sure there are plenty of you wondering why I would use these as examples for legitimate close protection personnel. Well, 1. To show that the criminals have trained shooters and weapons avalible 2. A lot of bussinesses overlap into the criminal world ranging from high-end jewllery to real estate. This is where you need to always do indepth due-dilligence on your clients, they may appear to be squeacky clean but, whats the the real reason they need your services! So, understanding a little about snipers and counter sniper operations is an essential part of your operational planning and preparations

Snipers

One thing I find amusing and annoying is that whenever there is a terrorist attack with an attacker using a long gun the media tends to immediately label the shooter as a sniper. There is a very big difference between a trained sniper and some idiot with a rifle and just because someone served in the military to some extent it does not make them a sniper. But, with modern weapons and a little knowledge the wannabe jihadist or anarchist are still a serious threat.

Whether your potential threat is from specially trained personnel outfitted with state of the art equipment or merely an individual with average marksmanship skills, armed with an off the shelf rifle and tactics acquired from YouTube, you need to have plans in place to minimize the threat and procedures in place for dealing with active shooter situations.

There are five general types of shooters: the military sniper, the trained infantryman, the trained marksman, the trained shooter and the untrained armed civilian. Tactically each group have their own application and operational styles, you need to understand a little how they operate to identify the threat you could be under and plan effective countermeasures.

- **Military Snipers:** At the top of the sniper field are those who have been selected for and passed military sniper schools that usually last anywhere from two to three months. Note, I said selected for... Candidates for most military sniper schools are usually selected to attend the courses after going through basic training and proving themselves capable soldiers within their units, to start with. In addition to long range shooting skills military trained snipers need to be experts in navigation, communications, camouflage, concealment and observation. These individuals are trained to select key individuals as their targets, stalk them and kill them at distance while avoiding detection.

- **The Trained Infantryman:** Infantry soldiers from professional armies should have no problems shooting and hitting a man-sized target at 300 meters (yards) with their service weapons in most weather conditions from a prone position. In addition to their shooting skills they are trained in camouflage, concealment, stalking and combat tactics.
- **The Trained Marksman:** Most law enforcement units and the like tend to have marksmen as part of their tactical units that should be trained in precision shooting past 300 meters. The law enforcement sniper schools last from 5 to 10 days and are commercially available to those who qualify. These schools put an emphasis on precision shooting at 100 to 300 meters, rather than the camouflage, concealment, stalking and combat tactics which are not needed by law enforcement units.
- **The Trained Shooter:** Most military personnel are trained to safely use, shoot, and qualify with a rifle on a regular basis, so they are trained to some extent, but the standards can vary to extremes. There are also the trained competition and recreational shooters who practice regularly and undertake professional marksmanship training but lack the tactical training. Hunters also fall into this category and tend to have at least a basic knowledge of camouflage and concealment.
- **The Armed Civilian:** These are shooters with little or no formal military or firearms training. You can see them all the time in the news reports from various international warzones. They have been given a rifle and ammunition and told which direction to shoot and that's about it. Their shooting is not accurate, they seldom deliberately target specific individuals, but they have high potential to cause casualties far out of proportion to their actual skill level at close and medium ranges.

Hopefully you can see from the descriptions above there is a lot more to being a real sniper than being able to hit a target at 100 meters and having your picture taken wearing a Walmart ghillie suit. What makes snipers extremely dangerous is their ability to be undetectable before and after killing their target; if you don't know where the threat is, how can you counter it? The art of fieldcraft is the bread and butter of the sniper; they can move undetected and have the discipline to stay virtually motionless and alert for hours, if not days at a time to get a shot, this is what sets the professional sniper apart from the trained marksman.

The Tools of the Trade

The typical range for a military sniper attack is 300 to 600 meters with medium-caliber rifles, but depending on the environment, weapons available and the skill of the sniper undetected shots from 50 to 2400 meters plus are possible.

Some of the main calibers for sniper rifles are:
- **.22:** Even though this is a very small caliber .22 rifles make excellent close-range sniper rifles, as they are small and easy to suppress. Within 100 meters with quality ammunition they should be able to deliver lethal head shots.
- **.308/7.62x51mm:** This round has been around since the 1950's and for many years was the standard round for NATO sniper rifles. This round, with the right weapon and shooter, can hit individuals at 800 meters and deliver harassing fire at 1000 meters plus.
- **7.62X54mm:** The Russian military first introduced the 7.62X54mm round in 1891 and it is still in use today with the Dragunov sniper rifle and the PKM machine gun. When fired from quality sniper rifles the round is accurate out to 800 meters plus, I say quality because there are many inferior copies of the Dragunov on the market.
- **.338:** The .338 Lapua has gained popularity as a sniper rifle cartridge and has been used extensively in the wars in Iraq and Afghanistan. In November 2009, in Helmand Province, Afghanistan British Army sniper, Corporal Craig Harrison, killed two Taliban machine gunners at a range of 2,475 meters using a L115A3 Long Range Rifle. This is the current record for longest recorded sniper kill. The .338 fired from military sniper rifles should be consistently accurate at 1500 meters but as you can see from Corporal Harrison shooting, it can reach out farther in skilled hands and in the right conditions.
- **9X39mm:** This is a Russian round that is used in the suppressed VSK-94 & VSS Vintorez rifles which have an effective range of 400 meters and has been in use by Russians and others since 1987. The 9X39 is a heavy, subsonic round that has excellent penetration qualities against body armor.
- **14.5mm:** The 14.5×114mm was developed in Russia during the cold war for heavy machine guns and anti-material rifles and is still used by many countries. There are numerous rifles chambered in this round with the average effective range of about 2000 meters.
- **.50 Browning:** The .50 Browning round was first developed as a heavy machine gun round in 1918 and today it's still in service internationally. In the Vietnam war USMC sniper Carlos Hathcock used a scoped M2 Browning machine gun to get a confirmed kill at 2250 meters. In the 1980's Barrett developed the M82 sniper rifle that has been used extensively in conflicts since then. These days they are quite a few manufacturers producing .50 sniper rifles for military, police, and commercial use. Sadly, many of these weapons have found their way into the hands of international terrorists. The average effective range of a quality .50 sniper rifle is about 1800 meters.

- **20mm:** There are several rifles on the market chambered in 20mm, the American made Anzio has a reported maximum effective range of 5000 meters. There are several bullpup 20mm rifles such as the South African Denel NTW-20 and the Croatian RT-20 which would be a more maneuverable option for sniper operations but at approximately 19 kg (42 lbs) without ammunition they are not really stalking weapons. These weapons are meant for targeting vehicles, equipment and buildings. Vehicle mounted or in fixed position these rifles could be used with devastating effects as their ability to shoot through most common building materials would render ineffective most cover from fire positions.

There is a lot more to distance shoot that just having a scoped rifle and ammunition, you must ensure the rifle shoots straight to start with. I was chatting with a friend who had spent time in Syria with the Kurdish YPG and he mentioned how a lot of the sniper rifles the Kurds had were not accurate, which is common in such settings. I expect a lot of the weapons were old and had been banged around which is detrimental to a scoped rifle.

Scoped rifles need to be zeroed regularly to ensure the rounds are going where you want them. If the optics are damaged or not properly fitted this can also lead to inaccuracy. The rifle's barrel needs to be in good condition and taken care of; Romanian rifles used to have very low-quality steel in their barrels, which lead to accuracy issues after minimal use. Ammunition needs to be of good quality, in many conflicts ammunition will come from various sources including the black market. Different ammunition will perform differently from the same rifle and old or damaged ammunition just might not be able to fly straight at all.

The weapon's sights are extremely important, and the weapon needs to be zeroed to the shooter. If the shooters eyes are good with quality open sights they should be able to hit a man-sized target at ranges of 200 to 300 meters. For precision and long-distance shooting optics are a necessity and on the commercial market there are a vast array of scopes to fit all budgets. The quality of night sights have drastically improved over the last 20 years and they have become freely available on the commercial market. Simple and low-cost optics will not enhance the performance of the average $500.00 rifle into the accuracy class of true sniper weapon, but these sights make the trained marksman a much more effective shooter at combat ranges out to 300 meters and beyond.

Many military sniper rifles are equipped with effective suppressors to either completely silence or greatly reduce the noise and muzzle blast of the weapon. Weapons such as the Russian VSK-94 & VSS Vintorez rifles have integrated suppressors on their barrels. Not only do suppressors reduce the noise of a weapon being fired, they also inhibit the task of trying to determine the location of a sniper.

Suppressors can reduce the maximum effective range of a sniper rifle but can be very effective when employed at less than 300 meters. Suppressors are available on the civilian market and are easy to manufacture, the legalities of ownership vary from location to location.

Countering Snipers

The first step in countering snipers is for everyone to be aware of the threat. This is where a threat assessment needs to be compiled and the realist threats need to be identified, if potential snipers are a threat then procedures need to be put in place. In general, operational planning for a sniper threat should always be considered to some extent. Not only should counter sniper procedures be planned for but they need to be practiced, your people need to be trained at least in the basic reactions to fire and the use of cover, preferably before they are exposed to the sniper threat.

When compiling your threat assessment check media reports and talk with locals and those with knowledge of your area of operations. You need to determine what the threat level could be; are there trained personnel, what weapons are available and what's their motivation and objectives.

When planning counter sniper operations, you need to answer four basic questions that will help you to assemble effective procedures that are relevant to your situation.

- What is your task and objective?
- What equipment and weapons do you have?
- What does your opposition want to accomplish and what capabilities do they have?
- What are the rules of engagement?

Rules of engagement are a very important consideration and can vary greatly, for example if you are caught up in an active sniper situation in an urban area in the US and you have a legal weapon on you, you cannot go blindly firing into potential sniper locations without positively identifying your target. Also, this puts you at risk of being mistaken for the active shooter and shot by police or other armed citizens. In a hostile or combat environment, your rules of engagement could be a lot freer but the limits of appropriate use of force need to be understood by everyone.

In many parts of the world people openly carry firearms and just because someone has a firearm it does not make them a threat. Also, just because someone is shooting, it does not mean they are shooting at you or being hostile. There is a big difference between someone in your vicinity shooting in the air and you being shot at with accurate and effective fire. You need to be able to determine the difference and plan your reactions accordingly.

Counter sniper procedures are mainly common sense and should be ingrained in most former military personnel with any hostile environment experience. Basically, if you can't be seen, you can't be shot, so limit your exposure, always make maximum use of cover, and move tactically. Remember, the sniper always has the initiative unless detected and is trained to wait for hours for a target or the time when your guard is down.

- Use concealed routes
- Avoid open plazas and intersections
- Stay away from and don't linger in doorways and windows
- Move along the side of streets, not down the center
- Stay in the shadows.
- When moving with others stay spread out and use bounding over watch
- Go around well-lit areas at night
- Never be silhouetted against lights, skyline or light backgrounds
- Move quickly and quietly across open areas that cannot be avoided.
- Make maximum use of cover and concealment
- Do not gather with others in large groups in the open
- Conduct all meetings, gatherings of personnel undercover
- Do not wear anything that could draw attention to you
- Do not establish routines

After your threat assessment has been compiled you need to survey the area around your location for potential firing positions that a threat sniper could use and routes in and out of those locations. Once identified those locations need to be monitored where possible, occupied with friendly forces, booby trapped or made unusable for a threat sniper. Clear any bushes or obstructions etc. that could be used as cover by snipers or inhibit your view of potential sniper positions.

Now in many urban and rural locations the potential positions for threat snipers will be endless, so your only option will be to limit exposure; if you can't be seen you can't be shot! Board up windows or put up screens to block the lines of sight for threat snipers. Canvas or plastic sheets can be used to make a dangerous alleyway or street crossing safer. In the long term, fixed positions, more solid barriers and defenses can be put in place such as sand bags or earth filled 55-gallon drums etc.

Here are some basic military considerations for counter sniper procedures that can be adapted to the civilian world. Not everything will apply to everyone and all situations

- **Cameras:** These days' surveillance cameras are widely available and can be used to monitor potential sniper positions. Hunters trail cameras can be placed in potential sniper positions and along the routes to those positions to help identify any potentially hostile activity in your area. Also, after a shooting incident to help identify the shooter. In hostile environments, special care needs to be taken when checking or retrieving cameras as they could have been booby trapped or the sniper could be waiting for you. Placing semi-camouflaged cameras around a property will let any potential threats know the area is monitored and can be a deterrent.
- **Drones:** Where weather conditions and budget allow, drones fitted with surveillance or preferably thermal imaging cameras are ideal for spotting potential threats especially in rural areas.
- **Observation:** Potential sniper firing positions should be constantly under surveillance and where manpower allows observers should be employed to monitor these positions for suspicious activity.
- **Patrols:** Random patrols should be employed to gather intelligence, identify hostile movements in your area and deny snipers access to firing positions.
- **Dogs:** Trained dogs can quickly search large areas and buildings for snipers who are trying to remain undetected.
- **Protective Clothing:** Ballistic vest and helmets will not always stop a sniper bullet, especially from large caliber weapons, but can significantly reduce the severity of wounds.
- **Armored Vehicles:** Whenever possible try to use armored vehicles.

Reaction to fire

Over the years, I have spoken to many security contractors, police and military personnel and find it amazing that when talking about their reaction to fire drills most of them just say they would draw their weapon and return fire etc. That's ok on a gun range but you need to take a few other things into consideration if someone is shooting at you! You also need to remember that if you are being targeted by a competent marksman unless you have detected them before they pull the trigger, chances are you're going to be dead or seriously injured.

Basics, moving targets are harder to shoot than stationary targets. It's a fact, it's harder to shoot a target that is moving than one that is stationary. So, if someone is shooting at you, do not stand still, run, and get into cover. Smaller targets are harder to shoot than large targets! If there is no cover for you, make yourself a smaller target and drop to a kneeling or prone position.

Following is an adaptation of the British Army individual reaction to fire drill. Some of this may apply to you and some might not- use this as a basic format. If you are serious about your personal security, you must put together a plan that is specifically designed for your situation and then practice it until it is second nature.

- **Preparation:** If you have a firearm it must be clean, serviceable, and well-oiled. Ammunition must be of good quality, clean and your magazines full. You must be properly trained and ready to deal with a shooting incident.
- **Reacting to fire:** The immediate reaction to fire is to move to cover as you are deploying your weapon and returning fire, if available use a smoke grenade or discharger to cover your movement.
  1) Dash- a moving target is harder to hit than a stationary target.
  2) Down- keep low and present a smaller target.
  3) Get into cover from fire.
  4) Observe where the threat is.
  5) If armed return fire.
- **Winning the fire-fight:** If armed as soon as the threat has been firmly located, you must bring down sufficient accurate fire on the threat to incapacitate them or force them into cover so you can extract yourself from the kill zone.
- **Re-organizing:** As soon as you have incapacitated the opposition or are in a safe area, you must reorganize yourself as quickly as possible to be ready for other possible threats. You need to re-load your weapon, make sure that you or anyone with you is not injured and inform law enforcement, emergency, or support services immediately.

Where the rules of engagement allow, suppressing fire can be directed at the general area of the sniper's location to force them into or keep them behind cover, so you can move to a safer cover or extract from the sniper's kill zone. Look for and shoot at objects close to the sniper's position that would cause ricochets and flying debris, such as brick, plastered or concrete walls. Also, you need to be aware of injuries from ricochets and debris when being shot at! In hostile environments and combat zones maximum use should be made of what light, medium and heavy weapons available.

Make maximum use of smoke dischargers where available and use the smoke to cover your movement. Commercially smoke signals are available from maritime stores as they are used for emergency signals on boats, also various smoke bombs are used for paintball and airsoft games. In a major city chances are you cannot carry firearms but can legally carry a couple of smoke bombs, if an active shooter situation develops drop smoke and bugout!

It is very important that you understand the difference between cover from view and cover from fire; you always want to locate the latter where possible. You need to consider which type of rounds will be stopped by the cover you're using. A table might be able to stop a .32 fired from a handgun, but a .50 round from a M82 will go through it and you.

If planning the defense for a building you need to consider what caliber of rounds the inner and outer walls can stop. Also, where large caliber rounds can penetrate walls you can expect bricks and plaster to splinter within the rooms and cause injuries. You also need to take note of any surfaces that would cause incoming rounds to ricochet within the building.

Cover from view means you can't be seen but can be shot and includes:
- Cardboard boxes and empty rubbish bins
- Bushes
- Thin walls and fences
- Thin tabletops
- Doors
- Shadows

Cover from fire means, depending on the firearm used, you can't be seen or shot and includes:
- Thick tabletops
- Heavy furniture
- Stone and concrete walls
- Dead ground
- Thick trees
- Various areas of a car
- Curb stones
- Re-enforced barriers

When you get into cover, you should always try to have an escape route and try not to get pinned down. When using cover as a shield, always keep low and fire or look around cover- not over it. When you are in cover and need to move, first select the next piece of cover that you will move to and move fast and keep low. Keep the distances between cover positions short. When you get behind the cover, assess your situation, where the threat is, etc. Keep moving this way until you are out of danger.

Hunting the Hunters

When a sniper threat has been identified and you have the trained personnel, weapons and are within your rules of engagement, you should take active measure to eliminate or capture the sniper.

Potential indicators that threat snipers are in your area could be:
- Personnel seen wearing camouflage uniforms

- Individuals in possession of binoculars, range-finders, and well-maintained scoped rifles
- Hearing single-shot fire.
- A lack of locals in an area before a shooting incident
- Reflections spotted from optical lenses
- Small groups of (one to three) local personnel wandering around or observing your location for no apparent reason.

To capture or eliminate a threat sniper you need to identify a pattern in their modus operandi such as:
- Time of day of sightings or shooting
- Direction of incoming sniper fire
- Location of threat sniper sightings
- Patrols would need to look for material evidence of threat snipers being in a location such as broken foliage, hide positions, cigarette butts, food, body waste, empty rounds casings or discarded equipment

Once a pattern in the sniper's routine has been identified, be it the location of a potential firing position, a route in or out of that position a covert ambush would need to be set and the sniper killed or captured. Note: Kill or capture operations need to be kept on a need to know basis, regular routines need to be maintained as not to alert the threat sniper or surveillance that they are being targeted.

Conclusion

Hopefully this article has given you an insight into counter-sniper operations and will enable you to draw up some plans and procedures to fit your needs and circumstances. Sadly, we all need to keep the threat from active sniper shooting in mind and be prepared to deal with worse case scenarios.

Reconnaissance Operations

I was taught and employed covert reconnaissance (recce) while in the British Army over 20 years ago in numerous environments. Since then I have taught and employed it while operating commercially in Europe, Latin America and Africa.

Personally, from what I have seen over the years recce training and operations are often neglected, I think because people would sooner focus on more exciting "direct action" training and operations. But without recce operations, accurate intelligence and proper pre-planning "direct action" operation usually fail.

Recce Operations

Reconnaissance (recce) operations are a necessity in all tactical operations as they provide pre-operations intelligence on locations, terrorists and can verify or deny a local source's information.

All recce operations need to be done covertly, the terrorists/criminals should not know you're in their area or what you are doing. Recce operations in hostile areas should be done in plain clothes and civilian vehicles, you need to blend in with the environment and population. Nothing tactical should be carried and if armed try to go with no government issue weapons. When I was working with vigilantes in West Africa in 2012 we detained a guy who we had spotted watching and following us while on a regular patrol. He was from a cultist gang and the clear give away he was a criminal doing surveillance on us was that he had nothing on him; no money, no ID, no phone, nothing; Just the clothes he was wearing. I take it he had the misconception the vigilantes would have stolen his possessions... Moral of the story, when trying to blend in with the local population don't overdo it or under do it!

Things that could need to be recced include areas for arrest operations, terrorist/criminal safe houses, camps, meeting locations, routes, ambush locations etc. in urban and rural areas.

For example, if recceing an area for an arrest operation some of the things to be considered would be:

1. Approaches
2. Team drop off locations
3. Team's surveillance / cut off / snatch team positions

4. Communications dead spots
5. Vehicle and pedestrian traffic
6. Any terrorist/criminal surveillance or security in the area
7. Friendliness of civilians to the terrorists/criminals; would they intervene to protect them
8. Safe arcs of fire and no fire areas
9. Any CCTV that is in the area
10. Escape and exfiltration routes
11. Etc.

Some things to considered if conducting a close target recce on a terrorist/criminal safe house could include:

1. Approaches
2. Surveillance and remote camera locations
3. Communications dead spots
4. Routes for walk by recce's
5. Terrorist/criminal surveillance and security
6. Lines of communications to the safe house
7. Any visible security or defensive measures
8. Any vacant buildings in the area
9. What vehicles are in or near the safe house
10. Does the building have electricity, if yes what's the source?
11. Where are the phone lines and is there Wi-Fi?
12. Where are the water sources and supplies?
13. Does the building have air conditioning?
14. What type of roof does the building have and can you access it?
15. How could you enter the building?
16. Types of doors and windows?
17. Form up positions for an attack team and cut off positions
18. Possible terrorist escape routes from the building and area
19. If terrorists are seen are they armed, how are they dresses and are they alert?
20. Etc.

Maximum use should be made of video and stills cameras on all recce operations, these days with cameras in cell phones there is no excuse for not getting good video and photos. Video and photos should always be analyzed after the operation as they could have picked up an important detail that you had initially missed. Pictures speak a thousand words so get good video and photos!

You have two ways of conducting physical recce operations; static observation posts (OP) and close target reconnaissance (CTR). An OP operation would usually take the form of an operative taking a position in a vehicle, covert hide or even a café and watching a location or area. These days this usually includes the use of monitored or unmonitored surveillance cameras. Over the last decade unmanned aerial drones have been used effectively for intelligence gathering and direct-action operations. As technology develops and prices fall drones should be an option in a all recce operations.

CTR operations take the form of operatives walking or driving past a location and getting as much information as possible on each pass or infiltrating a terrorist/criminal location. You must be careful not to use the same vehicles or operatives to often on CTR's as they could be compromised. All operatives should have a believable and checkable cover story for being in the area, how detailed you go depends on the operation. Very few operations are perfect, and you need to get the most information possible without compromising the operatives and potential future operations.

The basic principles of recce operations apply to both urban and rural areas. In say a rural environment a static observation location could take the form of a camouflaged OP in a ditch, a bush or dug underground etc. Where as in an urban environment a derelict building, roof top or garbage skip/area could provide you with a concealed observation position.

Observation Post Operations

Covert observation posts (OP's) can be put in place for a few hours or a few weeks. Operatives conducting OP's need to be very self-disciplined, be able to keep quiet, handle extreme boredom and very uncomfortable conditions for extended periods of time. The general size of the OP team would depend on the task; usually they are between two to four operatives.

The equipment required for the OP would depend on the environment and the length of the operation. Once in position the OP team would keep their noise and movement to a minimum, so that will mean they will need to carry in with them everything they need for the operation; food, water, communications and spare batteries etc. In hostile areas re-supply can be risky but on extended operations it will be needed, generally supplies will be dropped off and picked up a distance away from the OP.

On OP operations over 24 hours' team members would need to work out a rotation system for who is observing and who is resting, one operative would need to be awake at all times. If there is limited cover the OP can be split with an observation and supporting location, if the operatives are moving between both, extreme care needs to be taken not to be spotted. Operatives need to be dressed, armed, with important equipment packed and at hand at all times. If the OP is compromised the team would need to flee the location, they will not be equipped or have the strength in numbers to engage a large terrorist/criminal force in a firefight.

To avoid detection an OP needs to be perfectly camouflaged using such things as scrim netting and in a rural environment local foliage. Any foliage used needs to be replaced regularly as dead foliage would give away the OP position. Noise must be kept to a minimum, even a poncho providing overhead cover can make noise that's unfamiliar in the bush and can alert locals to your presence. Another potential problem are smells coming from the OP team such as body waste and food, which will usually be eaten cold due to the smell from cooking and the weight of cooking equipment. Body waste would need to be stored in airtight plastic bags, bottles and carried away with the team when they leave the position. The OP team cannot leave any ground sign of their presence as it can jeopardize any future operations.

OP's can be for logging and reporting or reactionary purposes. A logging and reporting OP will do nothing but gather intelligence on a target. A reactionary OP can call in direct action forces or perform direct action operation themselves. It all depends on the task at hand and the resources available.

When working in West Africa we deployed logging and reporting OP's into suspected cultist and criminal areas to initially determine the extent of illegal activity, the terrorist/criminal routes and meeting locations etc. In Latin America while working with tactical police units we have had operatives go undercover as beggars in high crime urban areas on reactionary tasking while surveilling narco and whore houses. The basic rule is there are no rules, use your imagination and remember that flexibility of action is essential for all counter terrorist/criminal operations.

Close Target Recce Operations

Close target recce (CTR) operations are extremely important and supplies the intelligence that is the basis for all successful direct-action operations. CTR's are where operatives will get close to or infiltrate a target area or compound to gain real time intelligence. This requires the CTR operators to be extremely stealthy and devious to be able to get close to the terrorist/criminal locations without being detected and compromised. If they are making an undercover overt penetration they must have believable cover stories, look the part and be able to speak the local accents etc.

The size of a CTR team will depend on the task. Our usual CTR team is two operatives with others in a support position. I will advise the use two operatives for a CTR team as they can move a lot more stealthily than a large team and can assist each other in an emergency. In a lot of situations, it is a lot more effective for a lone operative to get close to or infiltrate a targeted location, it goes without saying that the operative should be trained and experienced!

The equipment carried by the CTR team should be minimal, their job is to gather information, not to get into fights. Everything carried by the CTR operatives must be able to be accounted for in a cover story. Items such as voice recorders, high end communications equipment and cameras will immediately draw suspicion of security forces and terrorists/criminals alike if the operatives are searched. In many places high end equipment will just end up being stolen by corrupt security forces if it doesn't get you detained, which can cost you money and heighten the risk of compromising operations!

CTR operatives need to travel as light as possible and be able to move cautiously and quickly, if compromised by the terrorists/criminals they would exit the area with maximum speed and not engage the enemy. If pushed to action they must be able to end confrontations quickly and efficiently without civilian casualties, which can be detrimental to future operations.

Over the years we have worked with teams employing CTR's on meetings in 5 star hotels, rural safe houses and numerous urban and rural terrorist/criminal locations. Commercially we have employed CTR's in Eastern Europe on suspected locations of counterfeiting operations, in Central America while working with tactical police teams we conducted the infiltration of whore houses looking for drug activity, underage sex workers and gathering intelligence for future raids. When working with vigilantes in West Africa the main targets for recce's and infiltrations were drug houses, kidnapper's locations in the bush, and when raids were organized the politics started, but such is Africa!

Where time, manpower and the situation allows several CTR's should be run on a location by separate teams to ensure the operatives are seeing the same things! Inexperienced operatives can over exaggerate what they saw because they are nervous, or they want to impress the operations commanders. Facts need to be reported, not suspicions, opinions or predictions. Operational security must be understood by everyone involved, nothing about operations should be discussed with anyone not directly involved; lose lips, sinks ships!

The basic recce principles apply to all situations, but the core requirement is having disciplined and well-trained recce teams. Reece operations are essential and required to ensure successful direct-action operations.

Counter Attack Operations

Fundamentals of the Tactical Assault

- **Fast and Fluid Movement:** Stay low and keep moving, fluid team movement comes from training, training and training!
- **Maximum Use of Cover:** Always use cover, always look up, always cover your rear, never stand in open ground and never stay in open ground... Get to cover!
- **Accuracy of Fire:** Fire accurate and controlled shots, don't waste ammo, don't spray and pray, every shot has a meaning and target!
- **Flexibility in Arcs of Fire:** You will sweep your people, trigger control is gun safety... Always be prepared for 360 degree contacts and defense! Sorry, but the bad guys don't read the conventional warfare rule books!
- **Accurate and Sustained Suppressing Fire:** Don't waste ammo, suppress the targets with accurate and controlled fire. Get comfortable working and moving with close fire support, closer the fucking better!!
- **Maximum Aggression on Target:** If it's a threat or potential threat kill it... If you need to capture a target have the necessary non-lethal weapons deployed and backed up with lethal weapons!
- **Rehearse, Rehearse, Rehearse......**

Hostage Rescue Threat Assessment

1. Has the incident started?
   a. If no:
      i. What is the source of the information on potential incident, is it reliable?
      ii. What actions to counter or intercept criminals will you take?
   b. If yes:
      i. What has happened?
      ii. When did it start?
      iii. Where is the location of the incident? Get maps, details etc.
      iv. Who and how many criminals involved?
         a. Ex-partner:
         b. Work or college:
         c. Friend:
         d. Group:

    e. Unknown:
2. Are the criminals armed?
3. For what reason have they taken hostages?
 a. Publicity for a cause
 b. Mental illness
 c. Financial gain
 d. Crime gone wrong
4. What demands have been made?
5. Have any other police or security agencies been informed and what action have they taken?
6. How as the incident progressed?
12. Possible type of action needed? Lethal or non-lethal, covert or overt
13. What are limitations do you will have to work within?
14. Manpower needed:
15. Support needed:
16. Time for rehearsals

Consideration for a Building Assault

Study Area – Map – Arial photos
Recce Drive By (Film)
1. Routes in
2. Approaches
3. Passby
4. Counter Surveillance location / CCTV
5. Routes out
6. RV

Foot CTR
1. Routes in
2. Drop off
3. Approach
4. Location
5. Counter Surveillance location / CCTV
6. Sniper/OP locations
7. Routes out
8. Pick up locations
9. RV

Assault
1. Team & Kit
2. Briefing
3. Rehearsals
4. Cordons & Cut-offs
5. Distractions

6. Route in
7. Drop off
8. Approach
9. Entry: Covert, loud or other
10. Clear
11. Re-org

Withdraw
1. Foot: Routes, CS, Pick up
2. Vehicle: Routes, CS, Switch

Post-Op
1. Defense
2. Debrief
3. Disperse

Basic Counter-Attack Considerations

There may be situations if you are trained and armed when you will have to take aggressive action. For example, an ambush that does not kill all those in the kill zone or just disables your vehicles, to get out of the kill zone you may have to attack the ambush party. An attack on a residence where access has been gained by the attackers, the residents or security team must clear any attackers from the residence. An attack on a shopping mall or hotel where you may be visiting or staying an aggressive action may be required to evacuate the location.

This is very basic information and can help you establish your own procedures if you are in a situation where you have the capabilities for counter-attack options. This is based on basic procedures for close protection teams and can be adapted to most situations. You cannot learn the skills required for this by reading a book or this chapter, you have to learn to shoot and train tactically for these tasks. This section can help you establish your procedures; you won't become a Tacticool Ninja by reading this!

There are three fundamental elements to aggressive actions:
- Speed
- Surprise
- Aggression

For your action to be successful you must have at least two of the above elements

Mobile Counter-Attacks

The conventional military response to an ambush is to attack the ambush. In most cases an individual or small security team would not be able to attack an ambush, for to do so would leave a client or family members without close protection when the need is greatest. Also, an individual or two-man security team would not usually have sufficient weapons or ammunition to perform and assault.

The best means of attacking an ambush is to use a separate security team not responsible for the client's immediate protection. The counter attack team should consist of people who have received training in small unit tactics and have sufficient firepower to deal with all threats. It should consist of not less than two people, in one vehicle. The counter attack team follows the client's vehicle at a distance so that it will not become caught in an ambush on the client's vehicle but close enough to be able to an attack the ambush quickly. The distances the team will have to be from the client will vary due to terrain, traffic etc. The protective surveillance team/personnel can be trained and used as the counter attack team.

Actions on a terrorist ambush by immediate close protection personnel:
- Return fire
- Drop smoke
- Cover Client's vehicle and attempt to break out.
- Send contact report

When counter attack begins:
- Give covering fire.
- Remove Client from the killing zone to a safe location.

If the opportunity arises to escape before counter attack team takes action, and never endanger the client because of your concern for the counter attack team.

Actions on a terrorist ambush by Counter Attack Team:
- Move to killing zone at best speed
- Use lights and siren for distractions
- Debus and attack ambush or drive at ambush.
- Do not hesitate. Fast, aggressive action is vital.
- If Client has been extricated, do not attack ambush but cover and move to safe house or emergency RV.
- Weapons. Maximum use must be made of automatic weapons, grenades and CS gas etc.

Counter-Attacks on Buildings

A counter attack on a building must be mounted quickly; the longer the delay, the more time the attackers will have to fortify their positions. A counter attack plan must be made and, if possible, practiced.

The counter attack team should consist of at least two people, but not more than five; i.e. a team leader and two pairs. The team leader needs as much information as possible on the situation in the building. This could be obtained from civilians, locations security team, staff by the use of radios or cell/mobile phones or social media.

The information required includes:
- The number "of attackers.
- The description of the attackers.
- Method of entry
- Types of weapons and equipment used by the attackers
- Location of the client
- Physical state of the client
- Location of any family or household staff
- Overall casualties

Methods of Entry
- If restricted by protective measures use same entry point as attackers but only as a last resort
- Enter by stealth whenever possible.
- Enter at the roof or top floor whenever possible.
- Early contingency planning to identify possible means of entry.
- Secure the entry point.

Room Clearing
- Work in pairs.
- Clear the door.
- On entering the room IDENTIFY targets before engaging with fire.
- Check all hiding places.
- When room is clear, secure and lock the door if possible.

Progression
- Control will be difficult.
- Clear the building progressively; room by room, floor by floor.
- Stairs. Once taken, stairs must be held.
- Use fire and Manoeuvre
- Avoid confrontation with other team members.
- Avoid being silhouetted or illuminated
- Use natural and locations lights to your own advantage.
- Use sound to disorientate the attackers: 1) Alarms. 2) Sirens. 3) Concussion Grenades.

- Use of vehicles for approach and escape. 1) Must not spoil surprise. 2) Must remain secure. 3) Must not be put to unnecessary risk. 4) Consider for external lighting of the location

Action when building is clear
- Ensure that the Client is safe. Do not, however, remove them from a safe room.
- Check that all attackers are dead or secured as prisoners.
- Ensure that the perimeter of the building is secure. Secure the entry point(s).
- Decide whether to hold or escape
- Co-ordinate external agencies on their arrival.

It is unlikely that plans proposed before the event will be put into effect as envisaged. The plan must be carefully thought out and rehearsed by all members of the team.

Bombs & Improvised Explosive Device Incidents

My personal experience dealing with terrorist Bomb/Improvised Explosive Devices (IEDs) incidents started in 1989 while serving in the British Army with 4 Platoon, B-Coy, 1-WFR for 22 months in Northern Ireland; since then bomb/IED awareness has always been a part of my security procedures and planning. I have to say that it astounds me these days after numerous, well publicized IED attacks globally that many security and law enforcement professionals are severely lacking in realistic IED awareness.

If you are working in the center of a large city, like London, Paris or New York, or are working in the emerging markets, where bomb scares are not unusual, it is likely that you may get caught up in a suspicious package or actual IED incident. Whether your venue, office or residence is targeted directly, or it just happens to be on the same street as an IED, you will need to know how to react and should have procedures in place.

Improvised Explosive Devices are a threat to everyone and are used frequently and with great affect by criminals, cranks and terrorists the world over. If you follow international events, then you will see that there is a lethal bombing somewhere in the world almost every day. The basic IED can be made from commercially available materials that are sold over the counter in most places. Information on how to construct IEDs is available from military or survival bookstores, the Internet, former military, or demolitions trained personnel. The size of an IED can range from as small as a cigarette packet to as big as a large container truck.

IEDs can be disguised as virtually anything; this gives the bomber the advantage of being able to kill their targets without alerting them to the threat, giving the bomber a large degree of anonymity. IEDs can be used to kill selected targets or to kill indiscriminately. These facts are why the IED is often the favored weapon of criminal, cranks and terrorists the world over and is the most dangerous threat to security, law enforcement, military and the public.

In this article, I have listed some basic information on IED's and some basic guidelines for dealing with an IED incident. I also dissect the law enforcement response to the NYC times square car bomb incident in 2010. And after reading this article you should be a lot more knowledgeable and competent than those members of the NYPD who were in charge of the response to that incident, well more of a circus than a response!

Explosives

There are many types of explosives available on the market, all of which have differing characteristics, chemical compositions and properties. What they all have in common is that they can be extremely dangerous. I am not going to go into the details of explosive composition because you don't need to know it; it makes no difference if a device has Composition B or gasoline in it, it's an explosive device and can kill you.

There are two categories of explosives: high and low.
- High explosives such as Dynamite, Gelatin, TNT, RDX, PETN, C-4, and Semtex undergo a rapid chemical change upon detonation. This change is a transformation from a solid or liquid to a gaseous state. The change, which takes approximately one billionth of a second result in the gas rapidly moving away from the point of detonation at speeds of up to 26,500 fps in the case of C-4. The moving gas is the force that cuts steel, concrete and anything else in its path.
- Low explosives burn quickly instead of exploding. The best examples of low explosives are gunpowder and match heads. The burn rates of low explosives are usually under 3000 fps. Low explosives are usually more sensitive to heat, shock and friction than high explosives, which tend to be pretty stable.

Commercial and military grade explosives are available on the black market either bought from corrupt soldiers/police or stolen. Also, you need to remember commercial explosives are used in construction, quarrying and by famers and is available for sale form explosive distributors.

Bomb and IED Identification

Bombs and IED's can be disguised as virtually anything, so you need to identify weather you, your clients or location could be targeted for an IED attack. You need to compile a threat assessment and identify all the threats you could be targeted by, if IED's are in the threat assessment you need to start making procedures for dealing with an incident. You must remember when compiling the threat assessment to also think what other potential IED targets could be in your area, which if targeted could cause issues for you. I remember one client telling me that during the 90's in Colombia he booked into what he thought was a nice secure hotel only to look out of the window of his room to see it was next to a small military base, which at the time would be an ideal target for narco-guerillas.

At a personal level, you need to be aware and suspicions of any objects, cars, or activity in or around your locations that could be a cover for an IED. An unattended and out of place bag, an unknown car that has been parked next to your building or on an approach road to long, unknown people acting nervously etc. You must be aware and suspicious, but you must understand the realistic threats or, you will be seeing IED's and terrorists everywhere. Common sense is something which is lacking in people today in general but, as a security or law enforcement professional you need to be able to keep things real and not get caught up in what can be classed in many cases as group hysteria. So, at a basic level everyone needs to know what to do if they are caught up in a IED incident, how to deal with a suspicious object or in the worst-case scenario the aftermath of a IED attack!

Detecting IED's can be extremally difficult; there are many bits of equipment on the market that can sniff explosives, ex-ray bags and vehicles etc. These are all good if you have them, they are well serviced and maintained. As far as I know most of the "bomb sniffers" have to be regularly calibrated and have their filters changed... I remember visiting quite a few high-profile locations in Abuja, Nigeria where the gate guards were using such devices to check cars, I doubt if the devices had been maintained since being taken out the box, and I would be surprised if they were even charged up. I paid numerus visits to a very high-profile hotel in Abuja and even though you had walk through a metal detector it was clear if you looked at the power cable it was unplugged...

The best example of fake bomb detectors was the British Made ADE-651 that claimed to be able to detect explosives, guns, drugs, ivory and even truffles and was powered by the users' static electricity. You may laugh, but the Iraqi Government apparently bought £52 million UK pounds' worth of them. Its claimed that up to 20 different governments bought the fake device at £60,000.00 a piece... They were made by the British company ATSC, which was dissolved in 2013 and the company owner Jim McCormick was sentenced to 10 years in prison on fraud charges. So, if you use bomb detectors make sure they are real, are maintained and the people using them know what they are doing.

In my opinion the best thing for detecting IEDs and explosives are properly trained and handled sniffer dogs. Again, at a base level, the dog needs to be properly trained, looked after, and handled... I know of one company in UK that use to ask their guards to bring their pet German Sheppard's etc. on residential security details so the clients could see they had, what they believed to be handlers and trained dogs. I have seen Civil Defense sniffer dogs in Nigeria that were so afraid of the cars they were checking they had to be literally dragged to them. Always verify you're getting what you are paying for, of all industries the security and defense industry should be one of the most credible but, in many cases it's a scammers paradise.

The issue with using dogs and the man portable bomb detectors is you must get close to the potential device and within the blast range. This is a big issue if you are dealing with devices that could have been put in place just to draw security forces into and ambush or suicide bombers.

The Secondary Device

Remember: The Secondary Attack, The Secondary Attack, The Secondary Attack!!!! If one incident has just occurred then what's next; another IED, follow up ambush, ambush on those responding or ambush on evacuation routes??

An IED can be used on its own or in conjunction with other IEDs or weapons. Good bombers will always place a second device near the first device, in a likely control point for security forces or on an evacuation route from the blast area of the first device. The second device is to catch the personnel or emergency services coming to the aid of anyone hurt in the first blast, security forces dealing with the incident or personnel escaping from the first blast. Sometimes the first device is designed to go off for no other reason than to draw in emergency or security services or drive people into the larger main device.

This happened in Northern Ireland with the Omagh bombing in 1998. Irish terrorists called in the location of a car bomb to local police with the wrong address, this resulted in civilians being evacuated into the blast area of the device; 510 lb's of AMFO... 29 people were killed and over 220 injured... I have a good friend who's family lives in Homs, Syria where there have been too many car and suicide bombings to count. After one suicide bombing incident, the locals rushed to help the victims, one man came out of the blast area bleeding and screaming for help. When people started to pick him up to carry to an ambulance, he blew himself up killing several of the civilians who went to help him, he was a terrorist.

I was recently talking with a client/friend who had a relative working at a hospital in Orlando, FL on the night of the recent terrorist attack on a nightclub there. After such incidents, the security for the casualty receiving hospitals etc. needs to upped as they are a prime secondary terrorist target as are the responding ambulance crews. When republican Irish terrorists bombed Thiepval Barracks, Northern Ireland in 1996 they placed a secondary car bomb outside of the barracks medical center to try to maximize British Military casualties. Think about it, where will everybody he heading after a terrorist attack and if the terrorists murder the doctors and nurses who will treat the casualties? Terrorists do not operate by the same human rights laws they expect to be protected by!

You must always expect if an explosive device has been found, gone off or that there could be a second or third device somewhere.

Northern Ireland

Here are a few examples of how IEDs were employed by Irish terrorists; these are taken from when I was a teenager serving in the British Army in Northern Ireland in 1989 to 1991. There were many more incidents but at the time dealing with such things was the bread and butter work for the infantry battalions stationed in Northern Ireland.

- **9th of January 1990:** Olven Kilpatrick was murdered by terrorists in the shoe shop that he ran in the town of Castlederg, he was shot at close quarters. The terrorists left behind an explosive device in a shoebox set to detonate 30 minutes after the shooting, by which time security forces and emergency services were in the immediate area. Mr. Kilpatrick was an off-duty member of the Ulster Defense Regiment. Think about how many shoe boxes there are in a shoe shop! The device detonated and several Royal Ulster Constabulary (RUC) officers were injured, there were no further fatalities due to the fact that secondary devices were expected to be left at crime scenes and the area was evacuated.
- **15th January 1990:** A car bomb is detonated in the Village of Sion Mills and causes major damage to the RUC station that was unmanned at the time. The security forces had limited routes they could use to get to the village. A QRF team form Strabane, lead by at the time Cpl Lewis Weaver responded to the incident and on the way out spotted a suspicious white van along their route, it was noted and they moved on at full speed. The same van was passed on the QRF's return route and the info was reported. On further inspection, the white van contained 1000 lbs of AMFO. It was reported several years later that one of the terrorists involved in the operation "Bernard Declan Casey" was working for British Special Branch and had ensured the command wire was not connected to the device in the white van... It was expected for an IED to be placed along one of the routes into the village to catch the security forces entering or leaving the area. If time was available the routes would have needed to be searched and cleared, if time and helicopters were not available this would consist of the responding patrol in driving in at top speed if there we no foot patrols in the area.
- **1990:** A car is parked a short distance from the "Hump" security force base in Strabane with what appears to be mortar tubes inside. A security force cordon is placed around the car to secure the area and when the security force teams are conducting their clearance searches around their cordon points, a team finds an IED attached to a trip wire. Further searches of the

cordon positions turn up other IED's. The mortar tube in the car turned out to be a piece of drainpipe, it was a hoax that was used to draw security forces into the IED's that the terrorists placed in likely security force cordon positions.
- **4th May 1989:** Corporal Stephen Mcgonigle, a very respected member of 1 WFR, was killed near Silverbridge, South Armagh. A car was parked on the side of a country road in an area regularly patrolled by security forces. When the foot patrol spots the car, they check with their control room to see if the car is registered as stolen. It was not. The patrol saw nothing overtly suspicious with the car, so moves forward to check it. At least one of the team was carrying electronic counter-measure equipment that can identify and block radio signal form remote-controlled bombs. The bomb was not remote controlled it was detonated with a command wire. The three other members of Cpl Mcgonigle's team were all injured in the blast.

You should take nothing at face value and always remember the secondary device. Always be suspicious of anything that looks out of place, if you are in an area where there is an active IED threat you need to draw up pans and procedure of how you will respond if you are caught up in an incident.

Types of Device

Letter & parcel bomb
Up until the late 1990's the letter and parcel bomb was the most widely used of all IEDs. The bombers who use this type of device range from stalkers through to hard-core terrorists. The letter bomb gives the bomber a direct line of access to the target and affords the bomber virtual anonymity for themselves, as the device can be sent from anywhere in the world. As the name suggests, the device is placed into an envelope or parcel and posted to the target. Upon opening the device explodes.

Below is a list of things that should be checked for on any package that you suspect as being an IED. If you or your client is under a threat, all mail should be checked. If some of the following criteria are evident on a suspect package, it should be put through an x-ray machine to confirm or ally your suspicions. If you don't have an x-ray machine, then the suspect package should be placed in a safe area and specialist assistance sought. The package would have been knocked around whilst in the postal system, so it will be safe to move-just don't open it.

Letter and parcel bomb recognition check list:
- Were you expecting the letter or package?
- Was it delivered by hand (to avoid the postal system)?
- Is it uneven or lopsided?
- Is the envelope rigid?

- Is there excessive securing material such as cello-tape, string, etc.?
- Are there any visual distractions on the envelope such as company, official stamps?
- Are there any protruding wires or tin foil?
- Was there excessive postage paid?
- Was the address poorly written/typed?
- Any excessive weight?
- No return address?
- Any oil stains, discoloration, fingerprints?
- Any incorrect titles?
- Any titles but no names?
- Any misspellings of common words?
- Any restrictive markings such as Confidential or Private?
- Any suspicious postmarks such as Belfast or Baghdad, etc.?
- Is the address stenciled?
- Any holes or pinpricks, which could be to let out explosive fumes?
- Any smell of almonds, marzipan or perfume used to mask the smell of explosive fumes?
- Any mechanical sounds?

Incendiary devices

A simple form of this device can be made as small as a cigarette packet and be made from condoms and commercially available chemicals. When properly ignited, they will burn at high temperatures and are primarily designed to destroy property. Incendiaries require an initiator (flame or chemical action), delay mechanism, igniter and main incendiary charge. Incendiary bombs are usually used against shops and businesses for extortion purposes or say a lawyer's office to destroy case records before a trail etc. They can easily be placed between the cushions of furniture or among flammable objects, in the case of thermite, on or above machinery or vehicles, and timed to go off when the business is empty of staff, causing the maximum fire damage. This can also help to give the bomber anonymity.

If either your client or his business is under the threat of incendiary attack, the following precautions should be taken. A deterrent would be to install overt CCTV and employ high profile 24-hour security guards. The CCTV could, in the event of an incident, be used to identify the bomber but keep the videos in a fireproof container or if using internet cameras back everything up on the cloud. If the client's workplace is an office suite, then access needs to be restricted as much as possible. Visitors should not be left unsupervised, all none fire retardant furniture removes and all areas search at the end of the business day. Cameras should be placed in high-risk areas entrances/exits and outside toilets and all personnel entering the suite should be searched.

Blast bombs

This device can be made very small. A device can easily be placed in a take away food container or bag and placed in a trash can or pile of rubbish, this type of device is used to cause disruption and confusion. In the city of London, UK, in the early 90s, a spate of such devices placed in trash cans resulted in all trash cans being removed from the streets and the London Underground. These devices can cause great disruption and kill indiscriminately.

Realistically, there is very little that can be done to stop a bomber planting these devices in city areas. The device can be easily disguised and moved during rush hour. It would be impossible to watch everyone, let alone search them, dogs could be employed buy they will not be able to sniff everyone. Security cameras on buildings and in shops would be useful when trying to identify the bomber after the device has detonated.

Pipe Bombs/Grenade's

Pipe bombs are simply metal tubes filled with some type of explosives usually mixed with a type of shrapnel (nuts, bolts, nails) and detonated by various means. If put together properly they can be very portable, concealable, and devastating weapons. Military grade hand grenades are available on the black market and are again very portable, concealable with most with an effective blast radius of 10 to 15 meters. One incident that comes to mind is from when I was in Jos, Nigeria in 2011, where a church was attached on Xmas Day... A grenade were thrown at a church and the police office working security was shot and killed... Simple attack that took seconds and the attackers escaped.

You have to be aware of your environment and constantly assessing people and their body language, in high profile areas where the threat assessment identified a possibility of this type of IED attack extra security measures need to be put in place such as screens on windows etc. so nothing can be thrown in.

Undercar Booby-trap (UVB)

This device was a favorite weapon of Irish terrorist's groups when targeting off duty police and military personnel. The device is placed in a container such as a Tupperware container and attached to the underside of a vehicle using magnets, usually under the driver seat. The usual method for triggering the device is by using a tilt or vibration sensitive switch. The UVB enables the terrorists to attack selective targets. There is a risk of discovery involved when placing this device as access to the targets vehicle is needed. If the bomber manages to plant the device, it will kill and maim the occupants of the car if it is not discovered.

The best defense against the UVB is to deny the bomber access to the vehicle. If you are under an IED threat and the vehicle is secured in a garage, the entrance and driveway to the garage need to be physically checked before the vehicle is moved. There could be a device attached to the door of the garage or a mine in the driveway. If the vehicle has to be left unattended, the surrounding area needs to be searched and then the vehicle. Searching a vehicle for IEDs is a basic and important skill and needs to be practiced regularly.

Car and truck bombs

Car and truck bombs enable the terrorist to conceal and move large devices. The car bomb can be used against individual or indiscriminate area targets. All it takes is for someone to drive the vehicle to the target and leave it to explode. Against an individual this device could be placed along a route or near an entrance to a building that is frequented by the target. The device can be triggered by remote control, command wire or, if the target is setting a pattern, by a timer. A method of delivering a device to a high security area is to use a suicide bomber or force someone to drive the vehicle with the device in it. The latter was a common tactic of Irish terrorists. It starts with the intended driver being kidnapped or having his home taken over. The driver is then informed that if they don't drive to the device or to the target they and their family will be killed. If they drive the device, at least he has a chance of survival. The driver is then chained and locked into the vehicle with the device and he is told how long they have got to get to the target before the device explodes. The driver has little choice but to drive the device to the target and hope the security personnel has some bolt cutter on hand with which to cut him out of the car, before the device explodes. Nearly all front gate guard posts and check points in Northern Ireland in the day had bolt cutters available for exactly this situation. On 24th October 1990 our Battalions main base "Lisanelly Barracks" in Omagh was proxy bombed, the driver of the vehicle was cut out by the front gate guards. This 1500 lb AMFO device failed to fully detonate due a faulty detonator.

As I stated earlier in major cities you can get caught up in IED incidents without be a target, just in the wrong time at the wrong place. April 24th 1994, I had just landed in Johannesburg, South Africa and was at the main bus station waiting for a bus a to Durban and talking to a girl I knew there on a payphone. What I though sounded like a bomb was a bomb and killed 9 people just up the road and I am sure injured way more, but the positive things was, as I remember my bus still left on time.

While in Abuja and Jos, Nigeria late 2011 and early 2012 there were numerous attacks on churches. One car bomb attack in Abuja that killed 37 people; the car had been parked in the church parking lot for days before the attack but never checked or searched. A smile pre-service sweep by a trained search dog would have identified the device.

Improvised mines

These devices can vary in size and be disguised as virtually as anything. Their triggering methods are only limited to the imagination and ability of the bomber. In Northern Ireland, large devices were usually placed in rural areas in culvert, under roads, or perhaps disguised as milk churns or in bales of hay. In the conflicts in Iraq, Afghanistan and Syria IED's= have been hidden in animal carcasses. In urban areas, they can be placed in lampposts, rubbish bins or in vertical drain piping on the side of a building. To place a bomb into a drainpipe, the terrorist lowers the device into the drainpipe from the top and a command wire detonates the device. The command wire can go over the building or be laid in the guttering connected to a firing point out of the line of sight of the killing zone. In all such operations, the terrorists use youths as watchers. The child playing at the end of the street shouting to his friends could be telling the bomber you are in the kill zone.

Sleeper bombs

An IED can be placed in a position a month before it explodes. If it is known that at a certain time in the future you or your client will be attending an event, a function or staying in a hotel at a certain time, precautions need to be taken. In 1984 in Brighton, England, such a device killed five people in an IRA attempt to kill the then British Prime Minister, Margaret Thatcher.

Defense against car bombs & mines

To beat the area car bomber, one has to vigilant and suspicious. If a vehicle looks suspicious, then get it checked out. Security forces have an advantage over private security personnel in being able to check out the background (whether it is stolen or rented) of a vehicle very quickly. So, if you are suspicious of a vehicle, call the authorities and let them check it out; if you are unwilling or unable to contact the authorities, then just avoid the vehicle. For private security personnel: when the car bomb or mine threat is directed at your client, then precautions need to be taken. If there are limited routes in and out of the client's residence or office, then these routes need to be regularly physically checked. Any suspicious cars, recent digging or wires leading away from the road need to be checked out.

When the client is traveling to and from work, the routes must be varied as much as possible. All trips should be kept secret until the last minute and then be preceded by an advanced security team, which needs to arrive at the client destination with enough time to check out the area before the client arrives. When entering or exiting a building, different entrances/exits need to be used. If possible, use fire escapes and staff entrances. If the client is to stay in a hotel their room will need to be searched along with the adjoining rooms, if possible, and a check kept on anyone using the rooms. If the rooms are booked a while in advance, a check will need to be done on all building work and maintenance carried out in between the time of booking and the time of stay, as this work may have been used to cover the planting of a device.

Suicide bombers

Suicide bombings are not a new issue, back in WW2 the Japanese employed attacks against allied forces to great effect in the Pacific campaigns, but in recent years suicide attacks have become the hallmark of Islamic extremist's terrorists.

The Israeli security forces have been dealing with the threat of suicide bombings for decades and at a frontline level rely on training their police and military personnel extensively in reading and understanding peoples body language, to try to identify suicide bombers and eliminate them before they can detonate their devices. There is no politically correct way to deal with possible suicide bombers, luckily for the Israeli forces their Government understands their situation and supports their actions. This is a huge contrast to the witch hunts British Armed Forces have been subjected to over the past few years.

In the wars in Iraq, Syria, and Afghanistan the front-line troops constantly face the threat of suicide attacks from devices in armored vehicle to devices strapped to children. In the battle for Mosul the Iraqi forces have been dealing with an extremely complexes situation as every vehicle and every civilian could be a potential bomber.

Kurdish forces in Iraq and Syria abiding by rules of engagement advised to them by their Western trainers put themselves at risk constantly by giving surrendering and wounded terrorist the benefit of doubt rather than a double tap. The Kurds are seeking independence doing everything possible to fight a fair war against an enemy that deserves no quarter.

Form a security professional's perspective if dealing with the threat of suicide attack's you must understand you are going to take casualties, but you need to plan to limit the extent of the casualties as much as you can. A recent example is the attacks on the Coptic Churches in Egypt on Palm Sunday 2017, one surveillance video shows one of the bombers detonating his device at the security checkpoint, most likely realizing he would not get into the Church without the device being discovered.

So, at a frontline leave everyone needs to understand what indicators they need to look for in someone's body language that could identify them as a potential threat. From a planning perspective, procedures need to be put in place to limit the bombers access to target areas and limit the potential blast area at checkpoints etc. In the case of an attack.

Mortars

These days no-one seems to consider the threat from mortar attacks. Mortars can be improvised and I see no reason why terrorists should not be able to get military mortars and ammunition. Mortars and grenade launchers have been found in the arsenals of Mexican drug cartels and recently in raid on illegal arms dealers in

Spain, so they are on the open market. Improvised mortars were used widely in Northern Ireland, against Security Force bases (and on mainland UK against Heathrow airport and the Prime Minister's residence in Downing Street, Central London). They were usually launched in quantities of ten, from an improvised base plate mounted on a flat bed or high-sided truck. The mortars usually contained about 45 lbs of improvised explosives with a fuse time of 16 to 20 seconds and a flight time of 10 seconds. Their range was between 80 to 250 meters. The propellant was normally made from Sodium Chlorate soaked "J cloths". Each mortar weighed about 120 lbs and usually went straight through most anti-mortar screening.

Attacks were common in Northern Ireland, one of our (1-WFR) patrol bases at the "Hump" in Strabane was hit in 1990 when D-Coy was on duty, Clady PVCP was hit when A-Coy was on duty, luckily no casualties on both occasions. The Irish terrorists tried the hit the "Hump" again in January 1991 when 6 Plt, B-Coy was on duty, the terrorist tried to put the mortars in a location where a RUC patrol was having a tea break. After a quick exchange of fire where everyone missed the terrorist escaped but at least the attack was avoided.

Military mortars come in light, medium and heavy variations. I would say that light and medium mortars would be the most useful to terrorists as they are quite mobile. The maximum range of light mortars, 50mm to 60mm can be anywhere from 700 to 3500 meters when firing high explosive bombs of about 2 to 4lbs with rates of fire from 8 to 20 rounds a minute. The maximum range of medium mortars, 81mm and 82mm is up to 5900 meters with high explosive bombs weighing 6 to 8lbs with a rate of fire of 8 to 20 rounds per minute. The ideal targets for mortars would be busy airports, chemical plants, gas refineries and petroleum storage depots. The best defense against improvised mortars is to identify and dominate any likely positions that could be use as a base plate location to launch mortar attack, this can be done with CCTV or patrols. If the terrorists have military mortars you are going to have a lot of problems controlling an area of up to nearly 6km around your location. This could be why no-one wants to consider the threat from mortars!

How To Deal With An IED Incident

POLICE OR SECURITY FORCES SHOULD BE INFORMED AS SOON AS AN IED IS FOUND OR IF YOU HAVE GOOD REASON FOR EXPECTING AN OBJECT OR VEHICLE OF BEING AN IED. DISPOSAL AND DIFFUSION OF IEDS IS TO BE LEFT TO TRAINED PROFESSIONALS. DO NOT ATTEMPT THIS YOURSELF.

Everyone should know the basics for dealing with an IED incident. If you are working in or have a business in an area where there could possibly be and IED threat you will need to draw contingency plans for an IED incident. If you are traveling to a city where IED incidents occur, you need to know how things can develop and whether security forces know what they are doing or putting you and others at risk.

There are four steps when dealing with an IED:
- **Confirmation:** Confirm, to the best of your ability, whether the object/vehicle is an IED, taking into account the following considerations: Are you under a threat from IEDs? Are the objects seemingly out of place? Are you in an area where terrorists are operational? Is there a funny smell around the object such as almonds, marzipan or petrol? This is where your threat assessment comes in. An unattended bag in an airport will arouse more suspicion then an unattended bag in a bar or restaurant but both could be just as dangerous or just as harmless. If all unattended bags in bars or other public places were reported as IEDs, there would be hundreds of false incidents every day but one just might be an IED. If you have good reason to suspect an object or vehicle, then check it. The police and security forces should be willing to help you, if you give them good reasons for your suspicions.
- **Cordon:** Once a device has been confirmed, the area around it and roads leading to it needs to be cordoned off so no-one can access. It depends on the size and location of the device, as to how far away the cordon will be but a basic rule is that you should be out of line of sight of the device. This is because if you can see the device you can be hit by shrapnel or debris if it detonates. Think of the potential IED as a rifle barrel, if you can see it, it is pointed at you and has a clear shot at you, it can hit you. In the private security world, cordon preparations and duties would fall on the static/residential security teams etc. If an IED turns up at your residence, the RST, if you have security personnel, would have to deal with the initial cordon and clearing of the area. Cordon equipment needs to be on hand, such as cordon tape, torches, and maps of the area and communications equipment. Plans need to be made for the evacuation procedures and cordon points for the different types of device. All cordon and control point location need to be physically searched for booby traps before being set up, the basic search would be 10 meters around the position.
- **Clearing the area:** People should be moved out of the blast area of the device; the blast area depends on the size and location of the device. In some cases, depending on the size of the device, it may be safer to leave people in buildings and under cover, rather than moving them into the open. It would make sense to assign a location in your building that could be used for this purpose, and internal room with no windows would be ideal. When evacuating people, a route should be taken that is out of line of sight of the device; if the device explodes when evacuating personnel, flying and falling glass is a big danger and needs to be considered when planning the evacuation route, as is the threat of secondary devices.

- **Controlling the incident:** Control of all IED incidents should be handed over to authorities, as soon as possible. You need to brief the responding personnel as to where the device is, when it arrived, how it arrived, where your cordon positions are, whether there is anyone still within the cordoned area and where they are. You also need to pass on any relevant information of threats that have been made or suspicious incidents or people that have been in the area. Not only is this professional, but it could help apprehend the terrorists.

When a threat assessment reveals a threat from IEDs, a great deal of planning is needed. Whether you are a business owner, lone international traveler or a close protection team member, procedures need to be made for dealing with IEDs. Everyone in law enforcement, homeland security and the private security industry must have a basic knowledge of how IEDs work, the effects of an explosions and how to deal with incidents but, sadly they don't. These days basic search techniques and IED recognition is a necessity for all everyone, as IEDs are the most widely used terrorist weapon and will be for a long time to come.

Times Square Car Bomb, NYC, May 1ST 2010

After reading what has already been written in this article you should be able to pick out quite a few mistakes in the New York Police Department (NYPD) handling of the 2010 car bomb incident in Times Square in the City of New York.

The vehicle that contained the explosives was a dark blue 1993 Nissan Pathfinder sport utility vehicle with dark tinted windows, it had been parked on a busy tourist-crowded. People in the area noticed smoke drifting from vents near the back seat of the unoccupied vehicle, which was parked with its engine running and its hazard lights on. They also heard firecrackers going off inside.

A police officer approached the car and observed the smoke, canisters inside, and the smell of gunpowder. The vehicle was set ablaze but did not detonate. Upon arrival, the bomb disposal team used a remote-controlled robotic device to break out a window of the vehicle and explore its contents. The device's ignition source malfunctioned and failed to detonate the main explosives. Had it detonated NYPD officials said the bomb would have cut the car in half, and "would have caused casualties, a significant fireball and would have sprayed shrapnel, and killed or wounded many people.

OK, the U.S. had been engaged in the war on terror for 9 years, so do the NYPD and other agencies not know how to deal properly with a car bomb incident. It amazed me when I saw the incident on the TV; they showed the bomb squad defusing the device with crowds stood watching. Basic rule, you and cordon positions must be out of line of site of the device, if you can see the device you can be hit by shrapnel etc. If the device had detonated there would have been many un-necessary casualties from the stupid cordon positions alone. The car bomb was described as a crude device, so was it not taken seriously? My first thought if I came across a crude and amateur explosive device would be, where is the real one, and that the crude device was nothing but bait to draw security forces into a trap. I strongly doubt the area and cordon positions were checked for secondary devices. In the TV coverage you could see that roads at either end of the road where the device was located were still open and cops were milling and sitting around relaxing, a suicide bomber could have driven right through the cordon and blown up the bomb squad, you can't protect others if you can protect yourself! The NYPD's handling of this incident can be classed as very negligent and how you should not deal with an IED incident!

If you are in an urban area and there is a car bomb incident you should initially find cover, get into a building and away from windows. If a device goes off the shock wave can break windows for few blocks around it. You don't want to be on an open city street will glass falling on you from 50 stories up. When safe to evacuate the area use back allies and non-obvious routes and do not hang around to watch how things develop. This is because of the threat from secondary devices and because the first device may only be there to draw in crowds of onlookers or channel people into the main device.

Conclusion

So, hopefully from this article you can see that dealing with IEDs is a complex problem where generally the terrorists have the advantage. The responsibility for IED and Terrorist attack prevention is everyone's responsibility, not just that of the frontline security forces.

- Urban planners and the like are responsible for including basic security features in their designs be it for shopping malls or airports. Sadly, in places like South Florida U.S. security considerations seem to be the last thing on their mind; who's going to attack a beautifully designed airport anyway... Next you will be telling terrorists will hijack planes and fly them into buildings...!
- Those responsible for security planning need to realistically understand the threats they could be facing and be allowed to put in place workable preventive measure and responses. I understand that a lot of times security management professionals sadly have their recommendations for upgrading security procedures ignored by their senior management etc. But they must perceiver and make maximum use of the resources they have.
- Frontline security forces need the proper training, equipment, and workable procedures to do their jobs properly. Untrained and badly managed guards

or police and not only putting themselves at risk but also those they are meant to be protecting.
- The general public needs to know the basics on how to identify suspicious and report activity and what to if caught up in a terrorist attack. At a family level, there should be plans in place of what to do if there is a terrorist incident at a shopping mall or public gathering etc. Some simple knowledge and 5 minutes discussing plan and preparations can save lives.

Many thanks to former 1 WFR members Lewis Weaver (Moose) and Matt Trott for helping with details of the incidents for Northern Ireland.

Orlando Wilson

Orlando's experience in risk management business started in 1988 when he enlisted in the British Army and volunteered for a 22-month operational tour in Northern Ireland in an infantry unit. This tour of duty gave him among other things an excellent grounding in anti-terrorist operations. He then joined his unit's Reconnaissance Platoon where he undertook intensive training in small-unit warfare and also undertook training with specialist units such as the RM Mountain and Arctic Warfare Cadre and US Army's Special Forces.

Since leaving the British army in 1993 he has initiated, provided and managed an extensive range of specialist security, investigation and tactical training services to international corporate, private and government clients. Some services of which, have been the first of their kind in the respective countries.

His experience has included providing close protection for Middle Eastern Royal families and varied corporate clients, specialist security and asset protection, diplomatic building and embassy security, kidnap and ransom services, corporate investigations and intelligence, para-military training for private individuals and specialist tactical police units and government agencies. Over the years, he has become accustomed to the types of complications that can occur, when dealing with international law enforcement agencies and the problem of organized crime.

Orlando is the chief consultant for Risks Incorporated and is also a published author and has been interviewed and written articles for numerous media outlets ranging from the New York Times to Soldier of Fortune Magazine on topics ranging from kidnapping, organized crime, surveillance to maritime piracy.

Made in the USA
Las Vegas, NV
20 August 2021

28565552R00095